SINGING ON STAGE

THE UNIVERSITY OF
WINCHESTER

Martial Rose Library
Tel: 01962 827306

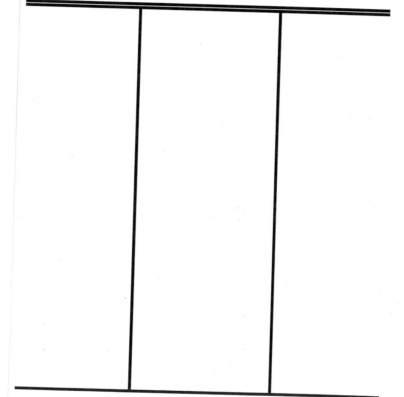

To be returned on or before the day marked above, subject to recall.

The cover photograph shows RADA Graduate Bertie Carvel as Miss Trunchbull in the Royal Shakespeare Company production of *Matilda the Musical* at the Cambridge Theatre in London's West End, a role for which he won the Olivier Award for Best Actor in a Musical, and was nominated for a Tony Award for Best Leading Actor in a Musical when the production transferred to Broadway. Requiring a complete change of identity and gender, the role is a perfect example of an actor's physical and vocal transformation into character.

Image by Manuel Harlan © Royal Shakespeare Company

SINGING ON STAGE

An Actor's Guide

JANE STREETON
AND PHILIP RAYMOND

BLOOMSBURY
LONDON • NEW DELHI • NEW YORK • SYDNEY

Bloomsbury Methuen Drama

An imprint of Bloomsbury Publishing Plc

50 Bedford Square	1385 Broadway
London	New York
WC1B 3DP	NY 10018
UK	USA

www.bloomsbury.com

Bloomsbury is a registered trade mark of Bloomsbury Publishing Plc

First published 2014

British Library Cataloguing-in-Publication Data
A catalogue record for this book is available from the British Library.

ISBN: PB: 978-1-4081-4547-0
ePDF: 978-1-4725-2067-8
ePub: 978-1-4081-4534-0

Library of Congress Cataloging-in-Publication Data
Streeton, Jane.
Singing on stage : an actors' guide / by Jane Streeton & Philip Raymond.
pages cm
Includes bibliographical references.
ISBN 978-1-4081-4547-0 (pbk.)– ISBN 978-1-4081-4534-0 (epub)– ISBN 978-1-4725-2067-8 (pdf ebook) 1. Singing–Instruction and study. 2. Acting–Study and teaching. I. Raymond, Philip. II. Title.
MT820.S942 2014
792.02'8–dc23
2013036183

Typeset by Fakenham Prepress Solutions, Fakenham, Norfolk NR21 8NN
Printed and bound in India

CONTENTS

This book is dedicated to Edward Brooks and Lyndon van der Pump.

The extraordinary legacy of their careers as singing teachers at RADA, the Webber Douglas Academy of Dramatic Art, the Royal College of Music and elsewhere is clearly demonstrated by the many successful singers and actor/singers throughout the profession who have been their students.

Both Edward and Lyndon have impressive links with previous generations of teachers who upheld the integrity of teaching methods which continue to fulfil the needs of modern-day actors.

Their encouragement and support of us, in our careers as singers and as mentors of our work as singing teachers, has been deeply inspirational and unstintingly generous.

It is through their example that we have learned to engage with our students in open-hearted collaboration, and they have inspired us to *work with* our students as opposed to *teaching to* them.

Edward and Lyndon have always encouraged us to bring our own experiences and personalities to our work and have continually affirmed in us that we should have the confidence to be true to ourselves.

It gives us great pleasure to offer these pages to them as a mark of our heartfelt gratitude.

PRELUDE

I was in Stockholm at the time. Sipping overpriced lager. Summer holidays in between second and third year. My girlfriend told me over the phone that the new cast lists had gone up for the autumn term, and I was apparently playing the Baker in *Into the Woods*. I was quite pleased. I didn't know the musical and I thought with a name like Baker it was obviously a minor role. (I wasn't really the most confident singer on the planet, so a minor role was ideal.) I went back to the bar and told my mates, one of whom was a farmer, and they all agreed it was probably a cameo.

Bit of baking, one quick song, then curtain call. Little did I know.

It's so easy to get vain when you're singing. That's what I found. It's so easy to slip into 'looking deeply affected by the song', and churn out some replica of a YouTube clip. RADA did away with all that. Warm up properly, get the breathing right, enough air flowing, enough things vibrating, and the song will do its job. My teacher used to say that singing comes from the same place as laughing or crying. She was right. And the effect it can have is overwhelming. Singing went from being something I was very afraid of, to something I couldn't wait to do, and the one-on-one singing lessons were often the best part of a week. You felt collected, alive, awake.

Watching my peers sing every term often gave me more goosebumps than the acting itself. Because if you can stick to the truth of what the song is trying to say, if you can hold onto that intention and almost forget that it's a song, it can be one of the most powerful tools an actor can have.

And needless to say, *Into the Woods* turned out to be one of the best stage experiences I've had.

Andrew Buchan
RADA Graduate

Actors should definitely learn to sing. It doesn't matter if they take to it or become especially gifted at it. Why? Because singing reveals you to yourself, exposing your innate voice.

Not just tenor, bass or soprano but tender, bossy or supple! Singing offers a moment to connect with one's own musicality (or lack of it) and to enhance it.

Of course this can only be true if taught well. I was very fortunate to have Edward Brooks, who really enjoyed matching songs to each student's capacities. I progressed from Cole Porter to Mozart – *Don Giovanni* … I still feel better if I sing to myself, 'Deh vieni alla finestra'. Edward allowed me to release my innate passion and power with Italian arias and Neapolitan sentimentality. 'Santa Lucia' fills many a shower cubicle in theatres all over the country!

More specifically, pitch, pause, breath, phrasing, containment and restraint over indulgence are all skills that benefit the spoken word, enabling one to develop a responsiveness to poetry and especially to Shakespeare.

A career spans many elements of self-use, on different media. If like me you are versatile, there is a grave danger that this can lead to facile work unless you've been exposed to a quality of aspiration, even if you can't achieve it.

Singing constantly challenges and reminds me of my unreached goals, and that's healthy.

It's not diminishing. It's humbling.

Henry Goodman
RADA Graduate

Soon after I first joined RADA I discovered that at the end of every term we were going to be required to stand up in front of the entire Academy and sing a solo. Singing lessons were provided, which turned out to be of a classical nature, often involving operatic arias. I was, at every level, horrified. I had never really thought of myself as a singer, let alone one who could stand on a stage and sing 'O Ruddier Than The Cherry' to a room full of my peers. But through a process of attrition, with each successive term the ordeal diminished a little, and by the time we all left we were taking this event in our stride and even offering up additional contributions to it.

Though never born to be the next Barbra Streisand, I came to be grateful to RADA's insistence on singing tuition for all. It forced me to overcome my intense self-consciousness, it consolidated all that we were learning about breathing and projection, and taught me much about that cocktail of concentration and relaxation that good acting requires.

Many years later, I stepped out on stage at the New York City Opera in front of three thousand people to sing 'Send In The Clowns' with a fifty-two piece orchestra. Though gyrating with fear I was just about able to function, and even – some evenings – to relish the heady thrill of singing Sondheim on Broadway. It was then that I had good reason to be immensely grateful to RADA for the importance it placed on singing as an essential part of our training.

Juliet Stevenson
RADA Graduate

Everybody sings. Even if it is school assembly or 'Happy Birthday' – off-key and out of tune.

A solo voice can also silence a room or sell out a stadium.

Somewhere in between lies the value of singing training for a drama student.

To experience those sounds, guided, controlled but free, is to be given just a hint of what might be possible when you open your mouth – to speak.

Alan Rickman
RADA Graduate

Carmen Vocis

Dedicated to the Society of English Singers

My soul is in my breath ; and with my breath will I lift up my voice in speech and song.

For my breath shall be turned into sound ; and I will pour forth my voice, even from the depths of my lungs.

And the sound shall be made true and steadfast ; by the security of my breath and the watchfulness of my sense that heareth from within.

My neck shall be as a temple around the sound ; and its spaces shall expand to adorn every cadence with fulness of tone.

The inner portal shall be open wide ; for in my throat there shall be no manner of contraction.

About the outer gate my lips and jaw and tongue shall play with all the supple freedom of a graceful dance ; and bring to life the beauties of my native speech.

Thus will I sing with my breath as with my soul ; and speak with my mind the simple language of my life.

For I am in my breath and in my voice ; and all my countrymen will hear me and understand.

W. A. Aikin

Foreword

INGING is the making of words more beautiful by means of music ; the singing voice is only one of the means to this end.

Half of interpretation lies in having the courage to leave things alone ; words are beautiful in themselves.

The singer's soul is in his breath ; the less he bothers his breath, the better friend it is to him.

The beginner hardly ever suffers from having too little breath ; nearly always from taking too much.

Music's soul is in rhythm ; in music each note belongs to, and moves on to, the note that follows it—rhythm never looks back.

There is an implied *crescendo* in the rising and an implied *diminuendo* in the descending note or phrase ; this is the first elementary rule on which phrasing is based. Like most other rules, it often pays to break it.

" Articulation is done with the tip of the tongue, the teeth and the lips." *(Dr. W. A. Aikin.)*

Speech is the foundation of song ; it is the bosom friend of the breath with which it has grown up from childhood.

Singing is hopeless without imagination.

Harry Plunket Greene.

If the words of the 'Carmen Vocis' were not present on the music stand in our singing lessons at the Royal College of Music, then they were always within arm's reach on the top of the piano. They were spoken by Dr Aikin, an eminent laryngologist and musical enthusiast, at a meeting of the Society of English Singers in London in 1916 to conclude a discussion on the state of singing and singing teaching in England. The form of the poetry is playful, in the style of an ecclesiastical psalm, but the content is truly profound and the thoughts within it are expressed with an eloquence, precision and economy that the authors of this book aspire to but could never supersede. It is the finest summation of the art of singing that we know.

The gentle and generous 'Foreword' is a response to Aikin's inspirational text by his colleague, the singer and teacher Harry Plunket Greene, and first appeared as the foreword to the publication *The Hundred Best Short Songs*, published in 1930. We have included this text as a reminder, to ourselves as well as to our readers, that our most important qualities as performers are inspiration and imagination, and that good technique helps unlock these without stifling our natural emotions and impulses.

INTRODUCTION

Some late-night texts after a singing presentation at RADA:

'Do you fancy writing a book?'
'On what?'
'On singing!'
'What for?'

Why do we need another book about singing?

Having taught at one of the world's leading drama institutions for a total of fifty-five years between us, we felt we might have some valid lessons to impart to actors looking to develop their singing, as well as having something to share with the contemporary student of singing who is seeking to further their knowledge and skill regarding the art of singing on stage.

It is a continual source of fascination to us how a kind of alchemy occurs when singing and acting are combined in such a way that both have equal value, and how in doing so they seem to yield more than the sum of their parts. Interestingly, as singing teachers, we have specialized almost entirely in working with actors, although we are classically trained singers ourselves.

At RADA we have developed a very particular approach, setting out to train actors to sing in a robust and flexible way, giving them a solid grounding with a classical focus. On the BA in Acting course, the training is maintained through weekly lessons over all three years of the course. Every acting student is trained as an individual, and the approach to teaching singing is deeply compatible with the approach to the training in spoken voice, movement and acting. It is a bespoke practice, which ultimately not only leads to our actors taking major musical theatre roles, but also gives them a skill set to draw on throughout their careers. Singing teaching for other, shorter courses draws from entirely the same model.

So we have written this book to bring together the experiences of all those, including ourselves, who have developed the craft of teaching the actor/singer at RADA, a development that we feel truly privileged to be an ongoing part of.

What kind of book should it be?

From the outset, we were agreed that this book should simply be a guidebook to the art of singing on stage. We have never felt that a book on this subject could be a replacement for a teacher or a course of study. For teaching and learning across the creative arts this is surely a universal truth.

In our way of teaching, we develop vocal technique and correct any difficulties that a student is experiencing as we see or hear them in the moment, and this very interactive approach cannot be easily recreated in a book.

Who would want to read it?

You do not need to have what may be termed 'singing talent' to benefit from this book. Many a trembling acting student has walked into our studios feeling they had nothing to offer and you may read comments from some of them throughout these pages. The fundamentals of the way we teach singing are equally applicable to all, whether you are beginning your training or established within the profession.

Maybe you did not realize that singing would almost inevitably come into the frame if you took your acting far enough. It is interesting for us that many of our students report back that even as early as their first professional audition they were asked to sing, and have observed that singing was vital to some of their subsequent casting.

We teach singing as much to strengthen and develop the vocal instrument as to give the ability to sing songs. Actors need to be able to match their sung and spoken sounds, so that the vocal interpretation of a character is organic and seamless.

The correct mental concept of singing and the physical conditioning and training of the singing instrument are crucial. Only when both of these are at the core of the process, and in equal proportion, can fundamental truths be reflected and spontaneous expression unleashed. These fundamentals are the common denominator of all good singing and are the real X Factor in great performances.

What style of singing do actors use?

Ours is not a book that seeks to provide a method appropriate to singing in a particular genre. There are many guides that deal in the specifics of how to produce vocal tone best suited to jazz, rock, contemporary, classical or operatic music. Rather it sets out ideas which aim to develop each student according to their individual attributes and to discover authentic, expressive and ultimately beautiful vocal tone as a product of the highest musical and theatrical values. This beautiful tone is then used as a basis to creatively and safely mould all manner of character choices, from a leading role in a musical to the drunk in a play who is supposed to sing out of tune anyway! Both must be executed with equal and appropriate truthfulness and be based on technical know-how.

At RADA and in other drama schools, music is constantly being composed for plays and presentations alike. All manner of material is written, from music devised by the students themselves to scores commissioned for specific productions. At any time, an actor may be asked to sing any kind of music, and ideally must be ready to do so.

How can we write this down?

One of our major challenges in writing this book has been terminology – specifically the semantics of singing terms. Communicating information about a physical act is complex, and writing it down places it at another remove, and one that is very finite. When teaching in the studio, words are a potent tool for us in communicating our craft. We use them 'in the moment' to elicit a response that might mean different things to different people. As an example, we may feel that to get our message across, saying 'see the tree swaying in the breeze' is more appropriate than 'see the breeze swaying the tree', or even 'see the planets creating the weather that produces the breeze that is swaying the tree'. Endeavouring to express all of these variations in written form might render the central thought unintelligible, reducing communication to pedantry. At the same time, reducing the description of our art to the 'matter of fact', in order to maintain correct semantic detail when describing singing, would be counterproductive.

Another issue that occurs when writing about our subject is the act of deconstruction; that is, the taking apart of something to examine and explore the various components. In teaching and learning singing, deconstruction is a hugely important tool, but there is only a certain extent to which it is useful for a student. Sometimes over-analysis can distort the individual components of singing in a misleading way.

Claude Debussy, the great French impressionist composer, once complained after hearing a performance of his music that the performers had 'carved it up like bits of chicken' and that as a result the whole had lost its essence. Consequently, deconstruction in our book is always considered with great care, for although it is fundamental to the understanding at a conceptual level, its usefulness varies in the moment from student to student as we deliver our work.

Throughout the book we have proposed listening suggestions – marked with a 🎧 symbol – which are mostly available on music apps or on the internet. We feel that all the singers included have qualities that transcend their genre and which have the potential to excite and move those who might not normally listen to that particular style of music. We hope that by listening to them they will serve as an inspiration to your work.

We have referred to the RADA training, and included other background and historical information in chapters at the beginning of the book, in order to contextualize our approach to teaching. We hope that by the time you come to the exercises and more practically orientated chapters, you may have a shared understanding of how we have arrived at them. Some of the chapters are long and contain mainly practical information, and some shorter ones are more conceptual. You may wish to read our book from cover to cover or to dip in and out, and we feel that it is important that you choose the approach that best suits your needs. As well, we are aware that there are many technical terms specific to singing, some of which will be familiar to you, and some of which may be new. Our Miscellany contains many of these words, explaining their meaning and elaborating on their usage.

So, welcome to our book.

We are fortunate to have been able to work with some of the most talented actors of our generation, and alongside esteemed teaching colleagues and directors. All of them have been important influences on our work, and with this very much in mind we offer this book, not as an absolute in any way, but as a reflection of where we are as teachers at this time.

The aims of this book are unashamedly aspirational, and we hope that it will be received as we present it, as a guide and companion for anyone who is interested in furthering the art of Singing on Stage.

1
A SHORT HISTORY OF SINGING AT RADA

Taking 'Six Degrees of Separation' as a rule, we are all somehow undoubtedly connected to an old Italian with a fabulous voice, and the authors feel that a potted history of our roots back to the beginning of the twentieth century might be of interest.

It is at the Webber Douglas Academy, or 'Webber D' as it was fondly called, where the connection between the modern-day drama student in London and the Italian masters of the voice was perhaps first made. The great singer Jean de Reszke (1850–1925) founded his singing academy in Paris in 1906. With his death, the academy moved to South Kensington when, in 1926, the singer Walter Johnstone Douglas and the pianist Amherst Webber founded the Webber Douglas Opera School in London. The former had been a pupil of de Reszke, and the latter the accompanist in his lessons. After about ten years, Webber D gradually transformed itself into one of the leading drama schools in London.

De Reszke was a handsome and charismatic Polish singer, who started his career as a baritone but, having studied in the Italian School with Antonio Cotogni and later Giovanni Sbriglia, became the world's foremost tenor. He sang frequently at Covent Garden and at the Metropolitan Opera in New York, was much admired by Queen Victoria and was a great friend of Nellie Melba.

De Reszke's first teacher, Cotogni, was himself one of the greatest singers of the nineteenth century and a favourite tenor of Giuseppe Verdi, the great Italian romantic composer. Verdi is said to have admired his warmth and strength of tone as well as his ability to connect emotionally with music, text and the dramatic situation.

In his later years, de Reszke became one of the most sought-after (and expensive) singing teachers in Europe. His teaching seems to have been a constant exploration for ideas that would serve all, but which allowed for individuality, as the following anecdote passed down through Edward Brooks suggests.

De Reszke was in an upstairs room feeling unwell with the flu while a student sang to an agent in the studio below. The student's intonation was poor, due mainly to the common instruction of the day, which was to push down vigorously with the diaphragm, forcing out the abdominal wall – this was meant to support and increase the vocal tone. The following morning when de Reszke came down again to teach, he calmly announced 'Le diaphragme n'existe plus!' (the diaphragm does not exist any more) – still a great tip for some modern-day singers and an insight into his personality and sense of humour!

An address to either the Society of English Singers or at the Royal College of Music by the singer Cuthbert Smith mentions that '... for days after that, all the pupils would be made to sing with arms outstretched to shoulder level, feeling as if they were "hovering like some great bird"'. The original, hand-written lecture notes of this address are in the possession of Lyndon van der Pump. It is a fascinating and revealing document!

Lessons were available at Webber D from first-rate singing teachers, one of whom was Cuthbert Smith himself. Smith had also been a student of de Reszke and, to help fund his study, had acted as pianist for other students during their lessons. The opportunity to observe de Reszke's teaching at first hand influenced Smith's own work and his subsequent development as a teacher. Eventually a disagreement between Walter Douglas and Cuthbert Smith over the fundamental physical management of the breath for good voice production meant that Smith left and was then appointed professor at the Royal College of Music.

In 1965 Webber D, on Smith's recommendation, appointed Lyndon van der Pump to be in charge of singing. He was joined by another Smith pupil from the RCM, Edward Brooks, a year later. In 1968 it was decided to mount a full-scale musical for the first time and *My Fair Lady* was chosen. It was a great success even in the tiny Chanticleer Theatre of the Academy. Musicals were just starting to become more popular in the West End and it was thought that drama students should be prepared and ready for the challenge.

In 1969 Hugh Cruttwell, the Principal of RADA, approached Lyndon and Edward to invite them to join his staff and develop the singing department there as well. Bringing with them another Cuthbert

Joshua Silver, Scott Karim, Jake Mann, Adam Nagaitis, Taron Egerton and Jordan Mifsúd in *Saturday Night* by Stephen Sondheim and Julius and Philip Epstein: RADA Production 2012. Photographer: Dave Agnew

Smith protégé and Webber Douglas teacher Beth Boyd, who was an established actor/singer, lessons became freely available to every RADA student, singing became a very popular activity, and they presented their first musical in 1970 – *The Beggar's Opera*. The trio helped many leading actors of the day, including Mark Rylance, Alan Rickman, Juliet Stevenson, Henry Goodman, Imelda Staunton and Jonathan Pryce, to make singing a real asset to their careers in the theatre.

In 1971 Lyndon was appointed professor at the RCM and was replaced by a pupil of his from the College, Darell Moulton, who has remained there until the present day. Edward was appointed professor at the RCM in 1981 and left RADA after twelve successful years. The authors, who were both trained at the RCM, Jane by Edward and Philip by Lyndon and Edward, joined RADA in 1985 and 1989 respectively.

We have been positively encouraged by each subsequent Principal and Director at RADA (Oliver Neville, Nicholas Barter and Edward Kemp) to develop singing and music-making in general. Within the singing training, students receive a weekly thirty-minute singing tutorial and a choral class. They also receive vocal coaching and participate in masterclasses, presentations and mock auditions, and in the third year there is an annual musical.

We usually stage the musical without microphones to help the students develop their vocal instrument, to improve projection of the voice, and to gain a better understanding of the relationship between singing and speech.

RADA Graduate Michael Peavoy (right) as Tony in *Billy Elliot the Musical*, by Lee Hall and Elton John, Victoria Palace Theatre, London. Copyright 2011 Billy London Limited. Photographer: Alastair Muir

Singing also takes place in many of the projects and plays that the students undertake, and can range from traditional Shakespeare Songs and sung Greek Choruses to German Art Song and music devised by the students themselves.

Our students enter the Stephen Sondheim Student Performer of the Year competition, with Michael Peavoy and Taron Egerton (seen in the photographs in this chapter) being two of the winners in recent years. We aim to prepare our students for every eventuality and, as graduates, see them perform in many genres including Opera, Gilbert and Sullivan and, of course, at the highest level in Musical Theatre.

I can think of few better ways for an actor to spend half an hour a week than to have a singing lesson. Producing sound freely and with feeling; being alert to rhythm and tempo; precision of diction and richness of tone: these are among our most valuable technical tools. Besides, to be alive to music is to let your imagination flourish.

Bertie Carvel – RADA Graduate

2
THE ACTOR'S WAY IN

Adam Harley, Peter Hannah, Verity Kirk, Francesca Zoutewelle and Freddie Stewart in *Six Pictures of Lee Miller* by Jason Carr and Edward Kemp: RADA Production 2013. Photographer: Linda Carter

Singing is fundamental for acting students because there's nowhere to hide. You will be revealed. Singing demands full commitment, love of language and complete exposure. Sing!

Che Walker – RADA Guest Director

Since the beginning of civilisation, singing has been at the heart of storytelling, theatre and dance; singing should be at the heart of everything an actor does.

Michael Haslam – RADA Guest Musical Director

'I can't read music.'

'I won't have enough breath.'

'Will I hit the note?'

'Do you want me to sing in head voice or chest voice?'

'I really like singing but I'm not very good.'

These are some typical comments that we hear from actors when they come to their first class. But the most common statement of all is:

'I'm not a singer.'

Within each of us is the innate ability to sing, and from our childhood we have encountered and engaged in singing in many day-to-day social settings. Hundreds of thousands of football supporters sing every week, and in all cultures, big occasions are often enhanced by music and singing. To sing 'Happy Birthday' is much more special than merely saying it. Singing unites people and can be a way of saying something that we are incapable of articulating simply with words.

Jenna Augen and Nick Hendrix (foreground) in *Company* by Stephen Sondheim and George Furth: RADA Production 2010. Photographer: Clare Park

Even though singing is constantly all around us, on our televisions and radios and available at all times on our iPods, we do not generally use singing as a mode of communication in everyday life. If we want to meet someone, we send a text to propose meeting for a drink, or email someone on an internet dating site. Quite a different approach from a lover singing a serenade under their beloved's window!

Although we all sing socially, at least to some degree, there is no reason why we should be able to competently use our voices on stage out of instinct alone. We must develop a process to enable this to happen, and our process is based on putting together a number of quite ordinary things in an extraordinary way. In our teaching, rather than blinding you with science, much of the initial work is related to things that you already know.

Many books on singing start with clinical pictures of vocal anatomy. Indeed, as an aspiring professional actor/singer, you may already be aware where your larynx and soft and hard palate are, where your ribcage and diaphragm are, and so forth. There are many books that describe this in great detail and you will find videos on the internet that show the internal workings of the vocal folds and other parts of the vocal mechanism.

Fantastic strides have been made in recent years in our technical and scientific ability to observe exactly how the body works, and this is a fascinating study. Technical aspects of singing, though, initially presented as sterile matters of fact, can become barriers for many actors, even when their purpose is the opposite.

Manuel Garcia, the most celebrated singing teacher of the nineteenth century, wrote an extremely technical book on singing but, when challenged, confessed that although he had written down all the science, he hardly mentioned *any* of it to his students!

In our process of teaching singing, we relate much of our technical work to the speaking voice as used on stage and also to your imagination. We do this not only because we believe that this is the best *way in* for an actor, but also because, as professional singers, we believe that this process creates optimum technical control and has the most potential to communicate feelings and move an audience.

At the beginning of your training, your perception of singing – what you think singing *is* – is almost certainly based on what you have heard *someone else do*. However, what an experienced singer is *doing* and what you are *perceiving* and *hearing* are two very different things.

As the aural recipient of singing, you are translating the singer's mental and physical act via the vibrations that hit your eardrum. As a singer you may discover that this is an entirely different process from what as a listener you had thought it to be.

Imagine a Martian seeing and eating cake for the first time. Also imagine his disbelief that this delicious creation is made from raw and individually unpalatable ingredients such as butter, sugar, eggs and flour. So with singing, the skills, both mental and physical, will probably be very different from what you are expecting if you have only been on the receiving end of what you consider to be good singing.

The Context

It is often useful in the beginning of the training to contextualize the work by gaining an understanding of why a playwright or a director might choose to use music in a play. It is often to change the mood or atmosphere, to create a sense of time and place, period or location. They might wish to underscore an emotional or dramatic moment and to provide a supporting narrative colour. They might use music between scenes to create a sense of continuity.

Actors have been singing songs in plays as far back as we can trace. Research shows that the plays of the Ancient Greeks included singing and instrumental music and the tradition of singing in theatrical performances stays with us. As a modern-day actor you will find yourself engaging with a plethora of different styles that have been developed through the ages.

The History

All actors are inevitably influenced by the history of theatre, and all students of acting research and explore historical context to inform and develop their work. For actors who want to sing, it is important to have an awareness of how music and theatre have interacted over time, and so we think that a brief historical overview might extend your wider understanding.

In the early development of music for the stage, one chain of events is clear. At the end of the sixteenth century in Florence, a group of true Renaissance Men, the Florentine Camerata, were looking to respond to the highly ornamented polyphony (music made up of more than one melodic line) that seemed to have overtaken the art of sung music. The Camerata included musicians, poets, noblemen, intellectuals and philosophers, who wanted to explore a new musical structure based on humanist values and for which they drew considerably on an idealized understanding of Ancient Greek civilisation. Research into Greek theatre, inspired by the scholar Girolamo Mei, introduced them to descriptions of the emotional and moral effect of theatrical performance upon the Greek audience.

Theatre was an important social activity in Athens and everyone attended performances, with the exception of women, slaves and foreigners! It was Mei's belief that Ancient Greek theatre was largely sung rather than spoken and so this led the members of the Camerata to the conclusion that this sung music must have been made up of a single melodic line with a simple accompaniment in order that the words should always be clear. This they called monody, and it was to be the basis for their further developments of the relationship between music and text.

As a result of their findings, the composers of the Camerata created recitative, a more spoken form of singing which allows the singer considerable freedom and where the natural rhythm and inflection of spoken words governs the music. Exploring the possibility of giving a musical setting to an entire dramatic text, they began to combine recitative with more lengthy and sustained moments of impassioned lyricism (arias) and with the further addition of choruses that often commented on the action – as in the Greek plays – they instigated *Dramma Per Musica*; this was really the birth of Opera.

At all times, the focus was on the importance and clear comprehension of the words. In one of the first treatises on singing, the composer and Camerata member Giulio Caccini declared: 'I should not praise that kind of music that does not allow the words to be understood.'

In taking Greek theatre for their inspiration with its powerful themes of love, sex, death, loss, abuse of power and the relationship between gods and men, the Florentine Camerata were convinced that such weighty human experiences needed a more profound visceral reaction in their portrayal than could be drawn from the florid and intellectual motets and madrigals of the polyphonists.

Looking from this distance, we believe that it was the desire to connect the highest values of Greek theatre to a new style of expressive music – itself growing out of a need to consider the text as inspiration for rhythm and melody – that expanded into the bel canto school that we talk about in the next chapter.

The Philosophy

How might ancient and more contemporary philosophical ideas give you another *way in* to exploring singing on stage? It may be interesting to consider how some early Greek philosophical ideas, which explored the relationship and balance between preordained destiny and man's individual free will, relate to issues for the actor/singer, who must make choices according to personal taste, capacity and identity, while honouring the constraints of the musical score and the *hard facts* that define their vocal instrument.

The hard facts (the things you cannot change) are the physical properties of your instrument, such as the size and shape of your vocal folds, resonators, as well as the muscular skeletal condition of your body. A baritone masquerading as a tenor or Lucy masquerading as Jessie (reference to Sondheim's *Follies* intended) will create problems down the line.

Not wishing to go into the region of self-help, we nevertheless think it is imperative to think well in order to sing well! We offer you our thoughts on how an actor/singer might think in order to fulfil the triple task of entertaining, moving and educating their audience while honouring the musical score. These were passed on to us by our teachers and inform our daily work, and form an attitude which we wish to pass on to our students.

- As a singer you are a story as well as a storyteller.
- Your story is as valid as anyone else's.
- Work with nature, not against it.
- Be in the moment.
- Don't let the bastards grind you down!

As teachers interested above all in exploring the capacity of each student to offer a unique and authentic interpretation within the structure of formal music, we hope these ideas act as provocations for thought!

The Challenge

As an actor, you need to be happy to rehearse in all styles, in the knowledge that you possess the appropriate dramatic language to explore the unknown. As a singer, you need that same confidence, and to be prepared to take on challenges of all kinds. In a career as an actor/singer you can be certain that you will be asked to engage with musical styles that are completely new to you, and you need to approach them with the same openness and eagerness with which you open the script of a new play on the first day of rehearsal.

Our brief outline of the development of western singing on stage from some of its earliest origins may be helpful for the actor/singer in understanding the breadth of tradition out of which the art of singing has evolved. From the plays of the Ancient Greeks to the evolution of Opera as a marriage of text and melody, it is clear to see a common thread which leads through such things as Gilbert and Sullivan Operetta to the more recent development of Musical Theatre. Popular music through the ages and music from diverse cultural sources have also played their part in developing theatrical music to the point where almost anything goes.

This has obvious parallels in straight theatre. On the London stage over the last ten years, there have been productions of *Macbeth* set in Japan featuring Noh Theatre movement and music, in Tribal Africa, in Mafia Italy, in modern-day Europe – in fact anywhere, it seems, other than in Scotland! An actor has to be ready to engage fully with whatever cultural, historical and stylistic framework the director has chosen for the play. In addition, many plays have unaccompanied music and we prepare our students to sing 'a cappella' for presentations and shows. At other times they may be accompanied by a fellow actor or actors on a range of instruments.

Ross Green, Beruce Khan and Brett Brown in *Poppy* by Monty Norman and Peter Nichols: RADA Production 2008. Photographer: Mick Hurdus

Raul Esparza – 'Being Alive' from *Company* by Stephen Sondheim – 20 February 2008, Edition of Great Performances on PBC

Raul Esparza gives an incredible performance of Sondheim's hugely challenging and climactic song, 'Being Alive', in a production where the actors all play instruments. This performance concept is becoming increasingly popular and there are now training courses for actor/musicians.

Fred Astaire, with Ginger Rogers – 'I Won't Dance' by Jerome Kern, Oscar Hammerstein II and Otto Harbach, from the film Roberta 1935
Could act, could sing, could dance rather well! Fred Astaire was more than a triple threat, he also played astonishingly good piano. At the beginning of this piece the octaves in the right hand and the stride bass demonstrate great pianistic skill. Astaire was a perfectionist and practised continually until he had mastered his work. The dancing at the end of this number draws to a breathtaking climax and the ease with which Astaire apparently achieves such extraordinary detail in his work is an illustration of true dedication.

The Core Training

In some ways it is easier to train oneself for singing in a specialized style than to maintain the flexibility required by an actor/singer, although every singer, whatever their style, knows that the bar is constantly rising. As an actor, you must trust your technical training, a training that should enable you to interact with many styles and yet still afford you enough control and skill to be able to surmount bigger challenges should the need arise. Some musical styles are highly specialized vocally, but in our experience, actors do meet these challenges with vigour, just as they might learn to play an instrument, work on a trapeze, develop a juggling routine or learn an accent or second language as they have been asked to do in recent productions at RADA. This is all down to having core skills, imagination and motivation to take on these challenges.

In singing lessons, it is our desire to show our students how to free their instrument in order to produce good singing and to set down neural pathways that will allow them to continue to develop physical and mental coordination and a subsequent vocal condition ready to meet great theatrical writing head-on. This is the whole point of our teaching. We use words such as *free*, *natural*, *authentic*, *centred*, *released*, and we attempt to communicate these concepts not only through words but also through our own state of being and our physical and vocal demonstrations.

Our technical work as presented in class and on these pages is therefore not centred on teaching you to make a sound like a baritone, like a soprano, like an actor, like an opera singer, like a jazz singer, like a belter, or like anything else. Your sound is thought of as a function of authenticity and your own free choice. When helping a student to build their vocal technique, we think that it is appropriate to put in place the deepest foundations possible. This is a bespoke process and occurs on a one-to-one basis in the singing studio and is very far from being academic or intellectual in its delivery.

From the moment a student first walks into our studio, we engage in a theatrical, vocally holistic and visceral approach to singing, even from the first exercise of using your mind to engage the breath to blow out an imaginary candle. We seek to engage within you all of the elements of artistic expression – intellect, imagination, body and voice.

In the course of writing this book, we realized that not only do we advocate being 'in the moment' as a performer, but also that we adopt this state in our teaching too. Ideas outlined in this book might be imparted to students at any appropriate moment in the training and some of the information we present may not be imparted at all.

The Path of Least Resistance

The most efficient way to achieve your desired result in singing is also the most natural. While a good sound can be made with any amount of unnecessary tensions, it will not be natural or what we call 'free' unless it is made via the 'path of least resistance'. The term is used to describe the workings of many ideal systems and complex processes and on a more fundamental level it is a universal law of mechanics. When your character's song exists because they have met an obstacle and cannot follow this path, then an interesting conflict will occur. This is the essence of many of our greatest dramatic songs – a perfect example is 'Let Me Finish' from *Tell Me on a Sunday* by Andrew Lloyd Webber and Don Black.

As singers we should be looking to achieve our character's dramatic *need* with the expenditure of the *least possible energy*. This is really what a good singing technique should be based upon. Least possible energy should not be confused with low energy. Your character, situation, genre and musical score might demand a great deal of energy, both mental and physical. This is when your technique must be applied very carefully to ensure that your character's conflict does not destroy your technique or your voice. The bottom line is that if you have been cast, it is *your* qualities that the director wants you to bring to the role, and these should not be compromised.

Your individual nature and true sound are paramount in singing and we encourage you to begin to work technically on your voice, knowing that in doing so you will become vocally freer, more confident in your abilities, and in the end more employable at the very highest level. After all, our purpose as teachers is to fit our students for the profession.

Before I attended RADA I was embarrassed about my singing voice. The weekly one-on-one singing lessons are as far as I can see unparalleled in UK drama training. Not only did they help ground me vocally, but I went from having a below average singing voice to playing a lead in a West End musical. There is no doubt that I wouldn't have achieved this without Philip and the singing curriculum at RADA. Outside of the musical theatre world there have been countless times both on screen and stage where having a foundation in singing has helped me enhance, keep or get a job. It's been a cornerstone to my career and has brought me much personal joy.

O. T. Fagbenle – RADA Graduate

3
BEL CANTO IN PERSPECTIVE

Kristin Chenoweth – 'Glitter and Be Gay' from *Candide* by Leonard Bernstein – Lincoln Center 2005
Here Kristin Chenoweth demonstrates her virtuosity, not as an end in itself or to show off, but as a gift to the composer's work, to the audience and to Musical Theatre itself. This is an example of coloratura soprano singing at its finest, where the fast passages and the stratospheric tessitura seem integral to the character and the expression itself (see Miscellany for coloratura and tessitura).
Breathtaking!

As singing teachers, we feel it is not necessarily helpful to be driven by one set model of technical work. Writing this book has given us the opportunity to consider what model of technical work we employ as singing teachers, and to confirm our belief that this must inevitably vary as we work with each individual. It is very clear that this is not a 'one size fits all' discipline and indeed it seems that the very mention of such a model might be a distraction from our desire to centre the work on the student's vocal freedom.

There are many singing techniques on offer to the aspiring student. Some are highly personalized, bearing the name of the originator of that given *method*. Others focus on a particular facet of singing or place more emphasis on how to sing in a particular style, rather than necessarily developing the voice.

However technique, when it becomes about itself in delivery, is in our opinion highly undesirable and even though a good sound can be made in all sorts of ways and by all manner of techniques, this may not facilitate communication and the art of good singing on stage.

We use a holistic and integrated approach, and while we agree that many techniques and methods of singing have certain strengths, we feel that the core ideas that *informed* the bel canto schooling are the closest to those we intuitively use to fully discover the possibilities of your voice.

Literally meaning 'beautiful singing' in Italian, bel canto is a term which describes a vocal training method, developed in Italy in the late seventeenth and early eighteenth centuries. It had a revival in the first half of the nineteenth century in the time of the composers Rossini, Donizetti and Bellini, and this neo bel canto school of singing was defined by a large vocal range, legato (smooth) line and florid passages, as well as by its expressive dynamic and declamatory qualities.

The essence of the *earlier* bel canto training was that it aspired to create the finest singing both musical and theatrical. We believe it was centred on the individual, was extremely thorough and pragmatic and that at each stage of training, enough time was allowed for vocal development before the next stage would start.

Very little was put down on paper by these early teachers of singing. Methods were, we presume, handed down from teacher to student. An example from the neo bel canto era is that Rossini – himself a singer as well as a composer – worked with Manuel Garcia (senior), for whom he composed the role of Count Almaviva in *The Barber of Seville*. The elder Garcia in turn taught his son, also called Manuel, who went on to become one of the most well-known of all singing teachers.

The musical compositions of Rossini, Bellini and Donizetti give us ample evidence that the vocal instrument was being developed in flexibility and range of expression hitherto unprecedented and many believe that this was the Golden Age of Singing.

Alfredo Kraus – 'Ecco Ridente' from *The Barber of Seville* by Rossini and Sterbini – 1987 film recording
Alfredo Kraus's astonishing coloratura and control of dynamics display an extraordinarily lithe throat, and his musical phrasing and legato is awe-inspiring. The speaking element is always present and the larynx is never manipulated from where it needs to be. This is some of the best tenor singing of all time, where operatic expression is not reduced to a form of show to please the public but is rather an expression of human capability as well as of theatrical and musical excellence. If you like this, also look up Kraus's recording of 'Je crois entendre encore' from *The Pearl Fishers* by Bizet.

Even in the early development of a training method, variations and contradictions are never far behind. If there is such a thing as a *pure* method, then there will be as many approaches to it as there are teachers – teachers quite understandably gravitating to the area within the method that most appeals to them. There was a Roman school, for instance, that started to value 'dark tone' as a direct response to a popular and successful singer employing such a technical effect.

Today, in the world of Musical Theatre, 'bright tone' likewise holds sway. The brighter American accent may be one reason for this. It may also be for some present-day sociological reasons that in certain genres of music, a childlike vulnerable sound has become fashionable for female voices. This focus on bright tone at the expense of using the full range of colours may be one of the reasons that some people use the expression 'it's very Musical Theatre' in a derogatory way to describe what can be a somewhat one-dimensional bright-toned delivery.

'Twas ever thus. Rossini himself was accused of allowing his writing for the voice to become so virtuosic that the singing had become more about itself than a vehicle for human expression.

We believe that, in essence, the original concept of bel canto was just a *truth of nature* and worked with the individual – almost as if it were in the first place an observation of the human condition rather than an imposed technique. Its true essence is simplicity, and its techniques need time and patience.

If we carry through our understanding of what we consider this technique to stand for, it supports our firm belief that the actor/singer needs to develop the full range of colours in the voice in order to make choices based on the specific demands of the production or performance situation that they find themselves in. No two actors will speak the lines of Hamlet's famous soliloquy in the same way, and we relish the different interpretations. So it should be with singing on stage, and each actor/singer should feel empowered to create an individual and spontaneous response in a performance situation, rather than premeditating a single rigid interpretation.

In certain students in our modern-day setting, *trying to be better* can be an overwhelming force which prevents their study being effective. Virtuosity properly discovered through physical freedom and fine-tuned coordinated response can become virtuosic for its own sake. Similarly, singing that is beautiful by force of its truthful simplicity must not lead to *trying to sing beautifully* as an aim. Concentration on working with the truth of what *is* and not what we *want it to be* in terms of vocal sound is what we believe to be the essence of bel canto.

Vocal demands made on singers have not stood still over the centuries – for example, pitch has moved higher, styles have changed, orchestras have grown larger, and venues have become correspondingly larger too. With the invention of the microphone and amplification, less technically developed voices have been able to remain small and vulnerable – even in the biggest space. Added to which, commercial recording has given us the ability to hear over and over again a definitive, *perfected* and *identical* performance, which has dramatically changed audiences' levels of expectation.

Unlike the students of today, the young students of the bel canto era did not have to sing in so many different styles. One of the potential pitfalls for the modern student of singing is in seeking to centre the work on the demands of the industry and feeling like they need to *do it all* and sound like everybody else! This mindset creates a pressure which is likely to put a cap on the potential for true and long-term vocal development. The apparent rewards for pleasing the public in the twenty-first century are becoming greater with the worldwide popularity of *X Factor* and the like and it is, of course, so tempting to produce karaoke performances of favourite singers.

Also, with ever more students competing for entry into 'the industry' and often more pressure on drama schools to deliver better results from less contact time, it is not surprising that this can lead students and teachers to go for the 'quick fix'. Sadly for the students, this is often short-lived, and we believe that for actors, this approach does not provide a stable enough foundation on which to develop authentic vocal performances.

Bel canto technique seems to us to not only to have stood the test of time but to also have a very contemporary feel to it. Jessie J, in our opinion, has a vocal instrument which displays many, if not all of the bel canto ideals and she does not allow performing energy to upset her natural balance and control. The late Whitney Houston singing 'I Will Always Love You' exemplifies perfectly the depth of meaning of the words *beautiful singing*. The *essence* of bel canto can also be heard in the songwriting of Adele, who writes beautiful simple melodies with a contemporary but bel canto feel.

Jessie J at fifteen – 'Get Here' by Brenda Russell – Best Young Pop Singer 2003
Jessica Cornish, as she was originally known, demonstrates a beautifully balanced core sound and incredible flexibility. Although she had been having singing lessons for quite some time, her natural technique seems nothing short of a force of nature. Her tuning is absolutely perfect in live performance and her phrasing is elegant and her legato superb. This is singing completely in the moment and an example of what it is to express yourself with tone and not make tone an end product.

Whitney Houston – 'I Will Always Love You' by Dolly Parton, music Video 1991 for Arista Records Inc. and Viacom International Inc.
This recording illustrates perfectly the importance of the word preceding the tone. Whitney's singing is heartbreakingly expressive and her superb vocal line, combined with the delivery of the lyrics, provides a masterclass in song singing.

Cynthia Erivo – 'Signal', written by Cynthia Erivo for That Grape Juice's 'The Splash', acoustic studio recording for (shft#live) 2012
Cynthia, a talented actor/singer and recent RADA graduate, performs one of her own songs. She sings in a contemporary soul idiom but her song has many hallmarks of simple bel canto expression. Her dynamic contrast and flexibility is evident throughout the piece and her expression is authentic and seemingly effortless.

RADA Graduate Cynthia Erivo in concert, 'Wired' at Concrete in Shoreditch London 2013. Photographer: Marcelo Nardi

Plato said that singing was nothing but speech with rhythm and melody in that order and not vice versa, and we agree. We do not look into the past with rose-tinted spectacles and place methodologies on pedestals. However, it is our belief that what we interpret to be at the heart of bel canto feels right for the transformative and expressive needs of our modern-day actors, and that it is the *true* quality which this technique promotes that can enable actors to stand out once they have been shortlisted for that leading role later on. Experience tells us that successful actors are authentic and wholly present when they walk into an audition room or onto the stage, and having bel canto ideals at your centre can only benefit you.

The incredible historic success of the bel canto school lay in its noble intentions, its logic, simplicity and its thoroughness. These are the aspirational qualities that inform our current work and feel most appropriate for RADA's leading position in actor training.

'What's hard is simple, what's natural comes hard' – Stephen Sondheim

4

THE ROLE OF THE
SINGING TEACHER

Our chief aim as singing teachers is to give you a strong technical vocal foundation which will underpin your working methods throughout your career. Having completed a course of study with us, the student should understand the process and be able to manage themselves well in the profession and come back to us only if they wish to develop still further, if they have a specifically difficult role or audition, or if the balance of their voice has changed. Otherwise one hopes that the graduate would be singing in some way – and therefore maintaining their technique – every day. At RADA we are in the fortunate position of working with students who want to learn, and elsewhere we work with professional and student actors who are committed to improving their skills and abilities. This energy and hunger for information brings out our best qualities and skills as teachers.

We firmly believe that the singing teacher should be or have been a singer. Our role is to help you develop your instrument and be your analytical 'ears'. A singing teacher who has trained and sung on stage should crucially have experienced the sensation of good singing and freedom of expression in performance situations and then be able to demonstrate and communicate this.

Demonstration of free tone is a very potent tool in communicating the sensation of energy and vibration in the body. At another level, a teacher must *show they know* in order to fulfil their inspirational role. When a teacher conveys the sensation of good singing to a student, he or she is probably well on the way to teaching him or herself out of a job!

As a teacher, one develops a feel for helping a student find their authentic singing voice which, although related to the speaking voice, is not always evident in it from the start. Sometimes it reveals itself when exploring the speaking voice the individual student uses on stage as opposed to their habitual usage, and sometimes it can be found and developed in exercises which elicit and explore more spontaneous and exclamatory utterances. Returning to a native accent, dialect or language can also act as a trigger.

Sensing freedom and authenticity in a singing voice is a complex multisensory activity. It is often easy to detect when it occurs, but it is hard to inspire in others if you have not experienced it yourself. This is one of the core skills which a singing teacher must possess.

The ability to empathize physically and psychologically with the student is also a key part of good teaching. If the student's technique is not quite right, we physically or vocally, perhaps even silently, copy their method, to see where or what the problem is stemming from.

A teacher who is also a practitioner will be able to understand and explain the experience of performing and the relationships with other colleagues and etiquette within the process. They will also be able to offer an insider's guide to such practical things as the effect that adrenaline has on a performer and, from experience, can tell you how to turn this to your advantage as positive energy. As well, they can talk from experience about the way in which you must pace yourself through the challenges of beginning to learn a role, through the rehearsal period and up to performance.

We tend to discourage the recording of classes. This is our personal choice; some teachers and students find it a useful learning aid. The exercises that occur in a class situation might be the singing teacher's response to your energy level and its appropriate usage. It is the response to a complex set of clues, both psychological and physical, and any exercise might be wholly appropriate in that moment but not so at a future point. The teacher is giving the exercise to elicit the feeling of a well-conditioned free sound and the desired outcome of the lesson is always to move towards this ultimate goal. Having achieved this, the teacher needs to direct the student towards a recognition of the sensation and then encourage them to acknowledge this achievement, seeing this state as being natural and not what they may have perceived as natural, which is often merely habitual. Appropriate work on exercises and songs should then be set (and recorded if required), based on regaining the sensation of free vocal usage.

It is the duty of the teacher to ensure that each student works within the boundaries of what he or she can achieve at every stage of their progress, while at the same time being aware that those boundaries should and will expand and thus the exercises increase in scope accordingly. In other words, the student should not be given a song or a set of exercises in which they are likely to *fail*. Offering analysis of someone's faults is the work of a critic and not a teacher. A teacher should inform the student of the importance of the work that they have done only after the desired outcome has been correctly achieved, and crucially not before the impediments can be overcome.

It is critical to be able to impart all the practicalities of being an actor/singer, drawing on personal and others' experiences. A teacher describing their own journey or citing examples of other students' journeys (without mentioning names, of course) can often have considerable impact. We all learn from experiences, both our own and those of other people, and these can be inspirational, even if the issues and circumstances are not exactly the same. Learning will be enhanced by sharing, and an open-hearted desire to collaborate.

Because singing is a kinaesthetic discipline, where each student has an individual process and response, a teacher should possess the patience to allow the student to learn from any mistakes they make along the way, and (with appropriate guidance) to discover for themselves how things work best for them. While close communication is essential, it is important also to have extremely professional boundaries concerning the details shared in a session. A good teacher's analysis of a student's particular problems is almost always compromised if the relationship becomes anything other than professional.

As teachers of a subjective discipline, we have to use a vast range of communication strategies to pass across to our students the individual messages that each requires. It is an individual, bespoke process, not one size fits all. There are many teachers that (with the best intentions) have settled on a single fixed path for their students. This approach inevitably suits some students very well but others not at all. In the long term, the most effective teaching is one which draws out unique vocal and theatrical expression from each student and does not seek to impose vocal colours and a performance style which can so easily lead to untruthful and unsatisfactory singing. The Latin stem of the word education (educo – educare) means 'to draw out' and is perhaps the antithesis of the scholastic or academic connotation of the word, which is 'to put in'.

Ultimately, the only real indication of a good teacher is to observe his or her students over a period of time and to judge their improvement. The development of a singer and of a teacher is very different. It is one thing to be aware of flaws in your own voice but it is an entirely different thing to be able to sense flaws in another's, and to have the knowledge and expertise to correct them. Because someone has a good reputation as a singer, it does not necessarily make them a good teacher. Once you've chosen a teacher, you need to give them a chance to work with you over a period of time, so that you can make a reasoned assessment of whether these methods will suit you.

There are two practitioners involved in the individual singing training at RADA, the singing teacher and the vocal coach. It is rare that you find a teacher who is equally experienced in performance both as singer/actor and accompanist/musical director. Our advice would be to go to an experienced singer for singing lessons and an experienced pianist/musical director for vocal coaching. As you progress in your training, it is likely that the balance of time spent with your singing teacher and your vocal coach will be something like this.

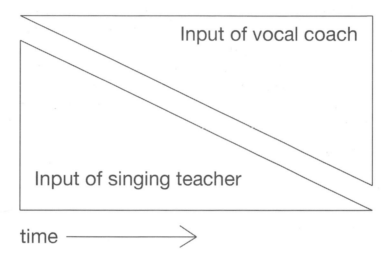

We will talk in detail about the specific role of the vocal coach in a later chapter, but at a fundamental level the goals of a singing teacher and vocal coach are the same, in that they are both intending to bring out the finest and most appropriate qualities in a student.

5

THE ROLE OF THE STUDENT

As an aspiring actress, you go to drama school with all the dreams of what you could be and the obstacle of your body and the reality of its lack of knowledge. When I listen to opera singers perform, I stand in awe and wonder at the human body and its ability to express in such fine detail. But my singing, voice and movement lessons at RADA were a forensic examination of my body, the resonance of each cavity, the power of my lungs, the openness of my throat, and within the strictures of discipline, the exquisite sense of freedom that was possible, of expressing oneself in a way I had never achieved before. My professional work has been more classical and contemporary than musical, but the memory of those lessons, and of the full potential of my body, are a touchstone to my work and my confidence as an actress and as a public speaker. The human body is an amazing and remarkable instrument, and I have one, all to myself.

Chipo Chung – RADA Graduate

You may be reading this book as an actor who has already had some singing lessons, or other musical training. It may be that you are new to singing, or that you feel that singing is not really your thing. We have taught many actors who felt that they did not have much talent for singing at the beginning of their training, but after a year of vocal development overtook the people that felt that they did, and we have had many students who have been told by teachers or parents that they cannot sing at all! We believe that everyone has a vocal instrument that is valid and worth training.

As an actor, it is counterproductive to worry that your voice is being judged in terms of its instrumental beauty. We come to the theatre to hear and see a well-rounded characterisation from an actor whose voice, body and psyche work in harmony, and in a good performance, singing may seem such a natural act that we are sometimes almost unaware that it is taking place at all because it is so integrated into the overall production.

If you are a beginner, we suggest that you have at least a term of weekly lessons from an experienced singing teacher to get your body, mind and voice coordinated together. Individually these components may well be doing the right thing by instinct, but you usually need to have someone to help you bring all three into line. In order to make teaching effective, the motivation to learn must come from the student.

In certain situations it is easy to burst into song and feel good about your sound (e.g. in the shower or when you have had a couple of drinks), but this is only at times when the mood takes you. Singing at a professional level or at student level when there are professional aspirations should be seen to be like taking part in an extreme sport where great attention to detail in terms of the technicalities is essential.

It is very important that you feel free to express yourself without fear of criticism. You need to find a teacher with whom you feel secure but not 'parented'. Although the status in the teaching and learning situation is quite correctly not equal on one level, equal status at a more fundamental social level will allow for more open dialogue through which the best teaching and learning can occur.

The student should feel able to understand the process every step of the way and it is absolutely essential that your teacher creates an environment where you are encouraged to ask questions if the process is unclear. The focus must at this stage be on the *process*, not the *product*. Athletes train, but do not constantly test themselves by trying to run a race every day.

'You don't fatten a pig by weighing it' – Chinese proverb

Much can be achieved by sticking absolutely to what is agreed upon, that is, the amount of time to practise each week – no less (and no more) than the teacher suggests. It is important to check in at the beginning of each lesson as to what has happened during the week and discuss honestly with your teacher whether you feel that your practising has been effective. Think through what has been learned and discuss what you feel needs to be continued or developed.

Good students make teaching seem second nature to us and it is hoped that a major function of this book will be to instruct you on how to be the best student possible! Crucially you should work towards being able to embody the physical sensation of voice and to be able to learn by recognising and developing freely expressive vocal tone, owning your own process and not just doing what you are told. The worst-case scenario for a teacher is when, on asking a student how it feels when producing their recently acquired excellent sound, the answer is: 'I don't know!' As a teacher, the answer one is hoping for will probably be quite individual: 'It feels easier', 'It's more exciting', 'It feels smaller', 'It's more physical' – even 'I'm not doing anything!' As a student you need to be able to recognize freely produced tone when you have achieved it, so that you are able to discover it anew whenever you are called upon to do so.

Other qualities which we feel are necessary for long-lasting success in any area are persistence, self-management and organisational skills. These will enable you to get the most out of what your teacher has on offer. Practise regularly! Practise even if you are not sure if you are doing an exercise correctly. If you are having weekly lessons in the initial stages, the teacher will more easily be able to correct mistakes at the next lesson with no harm done.

Ask your teacher how much to practise. Our commonsense adage would be 'a little and often'. The body needs to develop new habits, especially in terms of posture and breathing, which at the outset you can be aware of during most of your waking hours. Half an hour's practice a day would give you time to work on some technique, sing a couple of songs and work on some other material. When we were students we were also told 'one day off a week, one month off a year'.

As a singing student, you need to have an open mind to rethink or reconceive the process both technically and psychologically. For example, we often observe that if students have been trained to a high level as musicians previously, it is very difficult for them to put aside the idea that pitch or tone must be valued above all other thought processes. Perhaps some students have had singing lessons before and the working relationship with a new singing teacher needs to be established. When you have already achieved something particular with a previous training, it can be difficult to adjust to a new approach.

We encourage you to explore your unique artistic fingerprint and to recognize and to embrace your authentic vocal and poetic expression – in other words, to find your true voice. It is important that the actor/singer feels that they can take centre stage, and that the character they are representing is being filtered through their own voice, body and personality.

Students of Yoga practise postures and exercises that ultimately enable them to sit cross-legged on a mountain top and feel comfortable enough to meditate deeply without being distracted! Likewise, we study singing so we can walk on stage and express through music and words the whole truth of what we want the audience to understand, without being distracted by technique or lack of it.

You need to be willing to explore and research the music that you are singing. You will need to research singers, singing styles and composers, study musicals, plays and poetry and keep up to date with contemporary changes within the field. Alongside this research, it is important to be prepared to engage in additional activities such as movement, Alexander Technique, speech and articulation exercises, and even learn basic music keyboard skills and theory of music.

Singing well on stage often moves you to a heightened emotional and physical state which connects with feelings of anger, frustration, overwhelming joy and so forth. In song, your character sometimes

Lauren Swann, Bryony Hannah, Kyle Soller, Victoria Lloyd and Lottie Latham in *Little Women* by Jason Howland, Mindi Dickstein and Allen Knee: RADA Production 2008. Photographer: Mick Hurdus

communicates feelings which would otherwise be expressed through laughter, tears, screaming or shouting and as a student you also need to be ready to allow yourself to consider these emotions. As a result, occasionally there are tears or uncontrollable laughter in the singing studio. In fact, unless the student is open to allowing this to happen, progress can take longer. You are not *aiming* for these emotions – just *allowing* them if the situation arises. When we experience vocal freedom in the studio, it can very often channel our life experiences and emotional memories and when we least expect, the power of the writing, together with our concentration on this freedom, can trigger tears and deep expression without having to summon these up in a conscious way. This is a fascinating and exciting discovery and it can be empowering to allow yourself to express emotions in this genuine and vital way.

Eventually you will be able to recreate the sensation of good singing on your own and this independence is our ultimate aim for you. We will discuss this further in our later chapter, Practising and Taking the Reins.

I remember so vividly Jane very matter-of-factly telling me that it was perfectly normal in her classes for students to burst into tears or crack up into laughter – how singing is somehow closely related to those emotions. It makes you vulnerable. That's always stayed with me. Although I rarely sing in front of other people now, the training was invaluable as an aid to opening up and engaging your whole self and being present. It remains a very important part of my training experience.

Ben Whishaw – RADA Graduate

6
MAKING A PLAN – THE CONTRACT

The contract in this chapter is not only between student and teacher, but can be thought of as a contract with yourself. Establishing such a contract – normally verbal – with your teacher, at the onset of a training programme, is crucial to the teaching and learning process. If this stage is not properly negotiated the journey can turn out to be very rocky.

Each student will have a different balance of needs at the onset of training, although experience tells us that the beginner almost always wants certain specific aspects of his or her voice to improve: ease of production and vocal range – especially dramatic high notes, greater mastery over the break or passaggio – explained further in the chapter Ways we Work with Actors, breath control, and of course to build confidence. As some or all of these aspects begin to improve, new needs start to emerge as the artistry and expectation of the aspiring singer grows. Consequently the contract can and should be renegotiated periodically and an experienced teacher will be assessing the balance of needs and outcomes as the training progresses. It is really important, then, as a student, that you should think carefully about what you really need from your teacher and take time to express yourself fully right at the start of a training process. It is possible that there will be a conflict of opinion at this stage. Honesty about the objectives and the direction of your training is essential from both student and teacher right at the beginning of the proposed course of study and it is important that both parties are happy with the arrangement.

An outline of a verbal contract might be arrived at like this:

- What do you want from singing lessons?
- How do you see this happening?
- An appraisal from the teacher of your current vocal condition and how that relates to your ambitions.
- An agreement on a learning pathway.

If you are studying privately, you need to be honest with yourself about how much time and money you can put into the project. At the start of training, there is much to think about and reconsider in terms of day-to-day and minute-to-minute awareness, so it is best to commit yourself to the first group of lessons at a time when you can do plenty of thinking and be regular with your practice. There may be complementary activities that need to be engaged in or certain areas of your day-to-day life that need to be re-evaluated, and you must be honest about whether this is possible. Examples might include:

- Diet – times of eating may have implications for vocal health, for example acid reflux problems.

- Physical exercise – you may need to take more or, indeed, less exercise; for example, bodybuilding may produce destructive tension in the larynx. Perhaps aerobic exercise can be substituted – maybe cycling or swimming. It may be suggested that you try Tai Chi, Yoga or Alexander Technique, for example.

- Getting enough sleep.

Other peripheral issues may be discussed depending on the presentation of the student, for example a husky voice or bad posture may need to be dealt with before singing lessons should start. You should also raise any concerns at this point.

As stated earlier, the usual advice given to a beginner is that you should attend a term of weekly lessons and defer a next-step plan until after that. As a private student, it is better to save up and have a block of weekly lessons rather than stringing them out fortnightly, because a new routine needs to be established. Most of the work at this stage involves correct repetitive functioning and your teacher will need to instruct you on this regularly. In the interim, you may well go off on a wrong track and practise incorrectly. Although this should also be seen as a healthy part of the process, you need to be put back on the right track as soon as possible. It is only through trial and error that true progress will be understood.

It is rare that a teacher will promise any outcomes at the beginning of the training because while the method fundamentally stays the same, the application and outcomes will be different for every student and will be affected by your physical condition and mental aptitude in addition to your personal motivation. While reassurance from a teacher at the first lesson that they will be able to help is quite normal, a teacher that offers guaranteed results and outcomes is probably best avoided!

There is an old Italian adage that it takes seven years to make a singer. In the twenty-first century, the world of the professional singer is very different from that of the eighteenth-century Italian, but it still pays not to be in too much of a hurry, and to have realistic goals for the short, medium and long term.

7
FUNDAMENTAL PRINCIPLES – POSTURE AND BREATHING

Jamie Parker in *Guys and Dolls* by Frank Loesser, Jo Swerling and Abe Burrows: RADA Production 2001. Photographer: Mick Hurdus

Posture

Good posture for singing is a state of being where the body and mind are fully prepared to respond in a fine muscular way to musical and theatrical stimuli, both external and internal. Any pre-emptive tension that is not associated with this fine response would have to be undone in order to discover this state.

Many of the first exercises that we give to students are to reduce tension. These tensions may stem from insecurity when the student is working in areas in which they have little experience. Sometimes they are the product of habitual incorrect physical usage.

Trying to engage big muscle groups when singing is a considerable temptation for the beginner. If you have witnessed exciting and electrifying renditions of singing in any genre, you may have been struck by the physical tour de force that can be part and parcel of these seemingly all-consuming performances. It is hardly surprising, then, that you may feel that to throw energy – whether mental, physical or emotional or indeed all three – at a song must surely enhance the outcome. Also, a deep-seated and sometimes overwhelming desire to totally engage with a song that perhaps has had a big effect on you as a listener produces an urge to 'give it all you've got'. Yes, those performers may well be using big as well as small muscles in the final analysis, but their physical involvement will have been arrived at by using many aspects of themselves in a much more delicate and detailed way. Correct physical alignment is a fundamental principle of singing and we refer to it and work with it ourselves and with our students, every day.

People everywhere are becoming increasingly aware of posture. As our lives have become more sedentary, office workers are advised as to how their chairs should be set up to sit correctly at computers. Conversely, serious sports players and dancers often need to engage in activities such as Pilates to help their posture, as the exceptional nature of their physical usage pushes them to the other extreme.

Good posture is a state of mind as well as body, but often what is perceived outwardly as some sort of correct muscular alignment can be disguising a great deal of tension in the core muscular system and the vocal tract (the cavity/airway used in the production of vocal sound).

The human spine has two natural curves, and the head is quite a heavy thing to balance on top! This is one reason why it is easy for tensions to develop around these curves. Of course, these areas correspond absolutely to where we need the most fine muscular usage for singing; that is to say, around the neck and larynx, and the diaphragm and lower back. It is interesting to note that these areas also correspond to where we often talk about experiencing the physical symptoms of emotion: 'I have a lump in my throat'; 'I have butterflies in my stomach.'

F. M. Alexander was a Tasmanian actor who developed a technique to understand and overcome his own problems of vocal misuse. Broadly, the Alexander Technique addresses the psychology and physicality of release and a mental state of being in the moment – saying 'no' to habitual patterns and tensions triggered by an end-gaining mentality. End-gaining is the concept of trying to achieve an end product rather than focusing on the means. This is, in our terms, what we view as 'trying to sing' rather than 'singing'.

In other words, the principles of Alexander Technique apply absolutely here and reflect perfectly our deepest-held beliefs about what singing fundamentally is. We are fortunate to have this invaluable resource available to us at RADA, without which our teaching would be slower in the first instance and less effective in the long term and overall. Expert help from an Alexander Teacher is highly recommended for the serious singing student and superficial knowledge on the subject may be counterproductive.

In singing, making a vocal entry requires a great deal of muscular coordination. Also a finely balanced vocal entry requires too much for the brain to consciously process all at once. Therefore if your instruction to yourself at this crucial moment is one of conscious effort, this often results in a rather disconnected and non-artistic response to the material.

Starting to work on posture

Consider your physical reaction as you follow these instructions.

- Prepare to respond in your finest poetic, musical and artistic way to a stimulus which may be internal or external. You are preparing to respond with true ownership and will not be affected by any external criticism, real or imagined.

Have you noticed anything about your physical alignment and mental and physical energy?

- Notice the difference between this and your day-to-day posture and then your habitual response to preparing to sing. Stay concentrated in this state for a short time.
- Ask yourself when doing this:

  Do I feel ready?

  Do I feel tense or relaxed?

  Can I breathe freely?

- Imagine the attitude of the breast bone or sternum being that of energized self-confidence, not over-inflated, and not submissive in any way.
- Now, imagine another attitude in the back, that of lengthening and widening. Note that this is an attitude and not a physical test. That is to say, it is not the best lengthener or widener that wins the prize! Focus on the thought. Let your brain lead the process; do not manipulate your muscles.
- Now imagine your neck to be free from tension.

You may notice that you are standing with your weight equally on both feet, that your visual focus is at eye level and that your knees are not locked.

These are all indicators of an appropriate response and indeed this is moving towards a more natural alignment.

In a perfect scenario these instructions would be enough to induce appropriate posture in a creative and physically free student. Interestingly, most people react in a similar way to these instructions and enter a physical and mental state more appropriate to start singing, than if the instruction is to 'start singing', which normally produces a completely different state!

Initially, stillness of the body is important, in that you can begin to appreciate internal movements which you would be unaware of if you continually moved around. Ultimately the idea is that you will have complete freedom of movement while retaining full awareness.

Breathing

'The singer's soul is in his breath; the less he bothers his breath, the better friend it is to him' – Harry Plunket Greene

'If you say it is necessary to hold the throat when you sing, it is wrong – rigidity is the enemy of every art. To sing with the larynx in lithe unconscious freedom is the main thing. This depends, however, chiefly on a right control of the motive power, the breath' – the eminent English singing teacher, William Shakespeare (not the playwright), speaking eloquently on developing the voice that nature intended us to have.

Breath is the motive power which allows us to sustain our voice in many circumstances in our daily lives, and as RADA's senior singing tutor Darell Moulton often reminds us, this is the case from the moment a baby first cries. In order to make sound, the vocal folds (often called vocal cords) within the larynx are drawn together and if a sound that we make is constant or sustained, the breath is being controlled in some way.

Consider this: an early definition of inspiration was to blow breath into something and in doing so to give it life. The Ancient Greeks used the term inspiration to indicate something given spontaneously to man by the gods or, indeed, the muses who 'inspired' artistic creativity. The connection continues for the singer today. Ultimately your in breath should not be a considered, independent action. Instead, it should be motivated or inspired by the action or expression you are about to undertake; not premeditated, but drawn from your imagination.

In order to free the larynx to respond in an unconscious and flexible way to the imagination, we need to harness and utilize our natural functionality. This will not only allow us to sustain our voice in a more expressive way, but will also preserve the health of our instrument. The more expressive we are vocally, the more sustained our sound usually becomes.

Contrary to most beginners' belief, you do not need to be trying to get as much air into the body as possible. Pulling air into the body like this can create tension, and prevents correct supporting muscles from being engaged. This tension or muscular misuse can lead a student to incorrectly believe that they do not have enough breath to last a phrase, and so a vicious circle ensues.

Another common fault is attempting to aim the in breath into a particular area of the body. It is common for students to make an extra effort by raising the chest to inhale more air than they need. This creates a state which is anything but conducive to energized singing. The instruction to 'take a deep breath' can often lead to distending the abdominal wall in a rather unhealthy and unhelpful way, and can cause an equal amount of unnecessary tension. Ultimately, the in breath in free singing must be a reflex action in response to the music and poetry, not a predetermined muscular action. A full in breath, achieved technically correctly, is difficult but absolutely necessary in order to fulfil the demands of the great theatrical repertoire.

It is interesting to note that the instruction to 'get rid of the air' while vocalising, assuming correct posture is maintained, can sometimes result in the breath lasting longer than if you give yourself the instruction to 'conserve the breath' as you sing a note!

The reflex action of the breath

Think about your posture as described previously.

- Blow out all your breath as if to continually and gently disturb the flame of a candle – keep the throat as relaxed as possible.

Notice that we *do not* ask you to breathe in before you perform this exercise.

- Wait.

- Allow muscles around the abdomen to relax and air will flood in to the body creating 'the blossoming of emptiness', as the bel cantists described it. This is a reflex action.

- Wait.

- Breathe out all of your breath, making the sound you use to keep little children quiet in the silent section of the library – Shhh!

Say 'No' to tension in the throat. Connecting the breath to the thought is of paramount importance, so really 'Shhh' the children, rather than just making the sound.

- Wait.

- Allow muscles to relax.

Perhaps you are aware of the natural swinging out of the ribcage and the lowering of the diaphragm. You are not forcing or sucking air in.

Maintain the physical and mental state of good posture during the entirety of this short exercise. It is sometimes helpful to use a full-length mirror to check that the head and neck are well aligned and the position of the sternum is being maintained. Be mindful of any collapse or change of attitude in the sternum or spine, especially towards the end of the out breath. Again the mirror can be useful, as a habitual pattern of collapse at the end of the out breath may be only discernible by watching yourself.

Play with different thoughts on the out breath such as breathing on a mirror to mist it over. Simultaneously massaging around the diaphragm area with your hand can help to alleviate any tension.

The out breath should feel active in this exercise and the in breath passive or relaxed.

A little exercise we sometimes use is to pant like a dog and then slow this down, which can help to keep the mechanism flexible.

We cannot overemphasize the importance of the posture and breathing as described in this chapter. The fundamentals of this use of the breath, linked with correct alignment of the body are the mainstays of all of our work. Everything else that we do will be based on these crucial principles.

Try these breathing exercises in other postures too. The illustrations opposite show some suggestions.

You may well find that the breathing exercises are easier or feel more natural in some of these positions. Make sure you only do what is comfortable or possible for you. If you have done some Alexander Technique or Yoga you will already be familiar with some of these.

On stage you should always be using your body with an awareness of alignment and your theatrical or adopted physicality and vocal usage should always stem from a place of health.

All of the vocal exercises that we employ are in some way an extended breathing exercise.

The correct control of the breath is a fundamental principle in obtaining freedom and is all-important to our art. A technique founded on posture and breathing affords the actor the confidence to move into the sound world of the actor/singer with relish and curiosity.

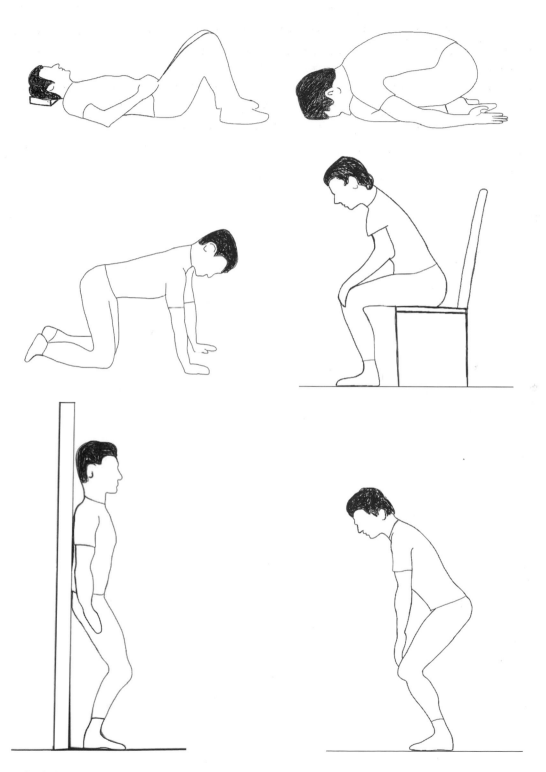

These physical positions, where the back is thought of as being lengthened and widened and the neck is free from tension, encourage the body to take a full breath

At RADA, we were always taught that breath is central to everything we do as actors. Singing and verse speaking complement each other extremely well in the training, since they both approach essentially the same challenge from slightly different angles – feeling and maintaining that strong connection to your core muscles, and controlling the release of air in order to communicate emotion truthfully. Sometimes the breakthroughs would come in singing lessons or performance, and sometimes they would come through verse speaking or other acting classes, but they would always feed other areas of the training when they came.

Gunnar Cauthery – RADA Graduate

8
WAYS WE WORK WITH ACTORS – EXERCISES

'One of the problems with teaching golf is that there are so many ways to play it well!' – Peter Alliss, the legendary golf commentator and teacher, on Bubba Watson's Masters victory 2012

So with singing, exercises can seem quite contradictory from teacher to teacher, being centred on different aspects of what is desired in the finished product, and according to the likes and dislikes of the teacher as different as chalk and cheese! Some exercises go into great detail about resonance, placement, passaggio, and so forth, and are often specifically pertinent to the style in which you want to sing.

The singing exercises that we employ at RADA tend to lead towards achieving a free and balanced core sound, so that the instrument is flexible enough for appropriate and vital transformation into character when singing.

Singing exercises are essentially an exploration of what your voice is and what it can do. Releasing what your voice is, and not what you think that it should be, seems to make it better in almost every case, not only in the moment but also in the long term. In other words, when we sing, we *sing* – we don't *try to sing*!

Unlike some dedicated Classical, Musical Theatre or Pop singers, who often come to us with a very strong idea about how they want to sound, actors often start with the attitude of being ready to explore and then develop what is already there. Counter-intuitively, lack of experience in singing can, in some ways, be an asset when beginning training. Some actors may arrive with vocal issues, but these are generally related to tension and our exercises loosen them up and help to release these tensions.

Singing should be done in a mode of physical and mental awareness but ultimately progress to a state of total absorption. This is the state of the natural or instinctive singer where the absorption is so complete that to them it becomes an almost unconscious and seemingly *non-muscular* activity.

Vocal exercises are extraordinarily difficult to describe, but invaluable to the process of learning to sing. We thought long and hard about including a recording with this book to demonstrate what we mean about some of our ideas, and we explored what it might contain, but we believe that it would be contrary to the way we teach exercises. We teach the whole sensation, not the sound of good singing. It is an individual process. To build confidence with one actor, we might start to sing an exercise using easily understood elements such as complete words. With another it may be more beneficial to introduce a more abstract deconstruction of the word, breaking it down into vowels and consonants. Sometimes we start with florid exercises, sometimes with a single note. We will choose the exercise that provides the most appropriate type of information that each student can use positively to structure their practice.

We spend much of our teaching time responding to students, as well as instructing them. We encourage our students to use physical sensation and an awareness of the building blocks of posture and breathing to give them the confidence and knowledge to move onto their next stage.

Exercises are used to develop the whole instrument. They cover elements such as vocal line, articulation, words, range, flexibility, dynamics, resonance, support, sometimes separately and sometimes in combination.

Singing is often described as tuned, sustained speech. In order to express emotion and thought on a larger scale, human beings often resort to sustained sound by screaming, shouting, laughing or crying. Even physical acts such as honking a car horn become more sustained, the more frustrated you become with another driver! Equally, pitch tends to rise in the voice when the emotionality of the thought is increased, until literally we are at 'screaming pitch'.

When you depress a key on a piano and the hammer hits the string, a specific pitch is sounded. The human voice does not work in the same way, so to smoothly connect different pitches it has to slide somewhat like a violin or a trombone. The voice is absolutely not a percussion instrument like a piano, whose notes go into decay the moment that they are quite literally 'hit'. It is interesting that most piano teachers and certainly those who taught us at the Royal College of Music would try to naturalize this effect by telling us never to hit a note on the piano but always to 'play' it, sometimes even to 'sing' it! Usually your singing teacher or coach will play exercises and melodies on the piano and you must be careful not to try to emulate the way this instrument works.

Claude Debussy, the pianist and French Impressionist composer known for his desire to connect with nature in his work and also for his extraordinarily colourful tonal palette, said that he desired the impossible, a piano without hammers!

Claudio Arrau at 88 years of age – 'Claire de Lune' by Debussy – 1991 recording
Listen to Claudio Arrau's 1991 recording of 'Claire de Lune', a piano piece inspired by Paul Verlaine's romantic poem. This is a good example of how, in the imagination and the hands of a great master, a piano can be made to 'sing' and to exhibit sustaining qualities that seem to defy its mechanical properties.

Singing specific notes which connect to each other with perfect smoothness but without obvious sliding, is in fact very sophisticated and a quality which is associated with singing of the highest order. This is termed legato singing. Our starting point in the exploration of the singing voice is in the laying down of pathways which will develop this much sought-after quality.

'Smooth runs the water where the brook is deep' – William Shakespeare, *Henry VI part II*

Exercises

Connecting breath to sound

Remind yourself of our posture and breathing exercises on pages 32 and 33, 'Starting to work on posture' and 'The reflex action of the breath'. Building on these, allow an exclamatory sound to attach itself to the out breath. Notice the inflection, or the natural rise and fall of the pitch of the voice and the lengthening of the sound.

- This may be one of happy surprise – Ah!

- Looking at a new baby – Ah!

- 'Now I understand' – Ah!

- 'Finally I understand' – Ah!

- A groan or a moan – Uh!

- Reacting to a small child's grazed knee in the playground – Ooh!

- Reacting to juicy gossip – Ooh!

Get creative! This is just a start.

Now slowly draw a small circle in front of you in the air with your hand, keeping your wrist and arm loose so as not to disrupt the posture of the sternum, neck and head and with the bottom of the circle at waist level.

Using one of these previous exclamatory sounds, allow the pitch to describe the movement. Keep the range quite small at this point, starting in a comfortable speaking range and returning to this pitch at the bottom of the circle.

Extend to bigger circles and wiggly lines, allowing the changes in inflection to be guided by the movement.

Explore the different sensations when a relatively large inflection in pitch is described physically by different-size circles. Do not be afraid to experiment. Why not use the sound made by a cartoon character falling off a cliff?

Now move on to develop this exercise by exclaiming melodramatic words instead of sounds.

- Tragedy

- Terror

- Infamy

- Horror

- Ruin

Avoid tension in the delivery and just let the voice respond to the word and the movement. Be larger than life. Perhaps you might feel a bit like a pantomime villain or a hammy Shakespearean actor! Enjoy the freedom of not having to summon up real emotions that may sometimes be associated with tension.

These exercises are a useful way to explore the full range of your speaking voice.

Another similar but more detailed exercise is to choose two adjacent pitches and pay close attention to how you are moving from one pitch to the next. For this you use a hand or finger movement instead of the whole arm.

Holding your arm out comfortably in front of you, move the hand or index finger up and down. Let the top of the movement be the higher of the two pitches and the bottom the lower. Begin slowly, so that you can experience the legato movement. Then try moving your hand quite quickly and let the pitch respond to this. Be aware that even when moving very quickly between two quite static positions you have to pass through all the positions in between. Move your hand at different speeds. The fastest might induce a vocal trill and if your inflection can accurately respond to this you already have a naturally flexible instrument.

Using your hands to describe sound relates the act of singing to movement. It is a useful visual aid and an external way to mirror what is going on in the body. It can work both ways, in that if you notice your hand being less than fluid, it tends to denote that the same is true of the breath and the thought.

These and other similar exercises are valuable because they coordinate body, thought, breath and sound. Slowing the movement down allows you the time to feel in control of your own process.

The singer always has choices as to how to connect one note to another. As your confidence in phrasing begins to grow, you will discover more and more options; however, legato will be the basis from which everything develops.

Give yourself licence to truly experiment with sound. As with any worthwhile scientific experiment, the results are not known at the outset, which is precisely why the experiment is being done in the first place!

'It is important to learn from the unknown as well as the known' – Nicholas Barter, Former Principal of RADA

Notes are in the head: The head hum

The fundamental difference between speech and song is that in speech, your tune pattern, referred to as *inflection*, is made up as you go along at the speed of thought, while in song you are using someone else's tune pattern or *melody*. The predetermined nature of melody makes it all the more important that actor/singers gain a physical understanding of moving pitch.

Adopt a good postural state and, with your mouth closed, start a small vibration. Imagine that this vibration is trapped in a small box, magically suspended in the head, and never at a level lower than the top of the roof of the mouth. This vibration is what we call a 'head hum'. You may find the simple instruction to 'hum' makes you wrongly push sound forward into your nose or mouth.

Let the box move up and down, allowing the pitch to move with it. Start by exploring a small degree of rise and fall. Moving a finger or hand at the level of the vibration to describe the movement physically can make the exercise more effective. The box can be thought of as a miniature passenger lift moving up and down through a building. Start with a non-stopping rise and fall and then perhaps let the imaginary lift stop momentarily at some floors (pitches) while on its journey up and down. Allow the sound to be quite atonal (musically haphazard) at this stage, as this can promote freedom and flexibility. You can move to more formal or tonal melodic patterns whenever you like. Atonality can always be returned to at any point if it helps you feel freer.

Let your hand continue to describe the movement. As you progress in this exercise, you may be able to find the upper floors of your building without conscious effort in the throat. Return to the ground floor and first few floors if you feel you are tensing your throat. Remember that the bottom floor should not be lower than the top of the roof of your mouth. Try a speeded-up stopping lift too! Practise the feeling of ascending and descending, 'stopping' and 'express'.

You can extend this exercise by imagining a greater intensity of vibration from within the lift box. Do not attempt to send energy up to the head to do this, just *will* the vibration to happen and intensify. This must be a consciously non-muscular activity. Try it sitting down if it helps you feel more relaxed. When you have become familiar with the feeling of this exercise, then you can play with more extended scales or arpeggios. When moving to more musical singing patterns, continue to move the hand gracefully up and down until you have gained real ease.

You can do this exercise for very short periods of time almost anywhere and anytime, because the sound you will be making is very small and unobtrusive. Any residual tension in the throat may be alleviated by simultaneously chewing an imaginary piece of gum!

A variation of this is to place a hand on the top of your head and be aware of any vibration while exploring this 'head humming' exercise.

The speaking element

The speaking element in the deconstruction of singing can be thought of as embracing all of the sounds that constitute human expression outside sung tone. It must not be thought of as merely a conversational quality, as it encompasses the whole gamut of expression including the extremes of joy, ecstasy, pain, fear, anger. Nothing should be denied. To colour your speaking element to *approximate* one of these emotions as a tonal aesthetic would be untruthful to natural function. As an actor you must be free to let your speaking element in singing respond as naturally as it would when expressing your thoughts in speech, from the most intimate pianissimo whisper to the most extreme projected shout.

Sing your lowest note and go up four or five small steps (semitones). This is the 'home' area of your spoken element, in terms of pitch. Developing a feel for this is very important when working on the singing voice.

The following exercises utilize a declamatory and legato style of speaking – imagine you are introducing yourself confidently to an audience in a medium-sized space. 'Good evening ladies and gentlemen.' Say it within your home area. Be aware of how this feels. Pay attention as always to your posture and breathing.

Using the declamatory tone you discovered when introducing yourself, speak a phrase or two from the words of a nursery rhyme (e.g. Baa, baa, black sheep, Have you any wool?) or you might use part of the 'Carmen Vocis' in our 'Prelude' or perhaps count in various languages. Changing the language can be very positive, as the variation not only keeps the exercise fresh but can be creatively stimulating. A small natural pitch inflection or movement helps to keep the tone natural.

Move your hand slowly away from you, palm down, on a horizontal plane at waist level while speaking, describing any inflection with your hand. Be aware of any vibration in the chest area. Place your other hand on your chest if you do not sense any resonance at first. Every voice, no matter how light or heavy, should possess a certain depth. Vocal depth should not be thought of as being synonymous with low notes or low voices but it is a quality or texture necessary to achieve balance in every voice.

Try various degrees of slow-motion speaking to explore the feel of the vibration in the chest. Extend every syllable so that you can appreciate the vibration of each one. The smooth movement of the hand at this stage helps to develop a feel for sustaining and legato. Feel free to allow the moving hand to lead you forward into a slow walk.

Let us consider a deconstruction of the words.

An exact pronunciation is not the purpose of this exercise so the phonetic breakdown below is quite general.

So one, two, three, four, five can be thought of as

Wuh_____ntoo_____three_____faw_____fah_____iv

The underscoring represents the lengthening of the English vowel but does not represent the pitch, which in this exercise should have gentle inflection and not be monotone, as this tends to cause tension. A monotone is in fact singing and so a monotone is not the same as speaking.

Moving on, A, B, C becomes

Eh_____ibee_____see_____

Notice how in English certain syllables are made up of more than one vowel. These are known as diphthongs. This can make singing in English quite a challenge.

Notice the movement between the vowels in these words.

From ah to i in mine
From eh to i in main

You can see that just as in moving smoothly from note to note in the earlier exercise, in transitioning from vowel to vowel you have to go through all the positions in between. The first vowel should be sustained for as long as the music demands, but the transition to the second vowel happens at a spoken speed appropriate to the text, not faster and not slower.

Now speak the words of a nursery rhyme, elongating the vowels.

Twi_____ngkuh_____ltwi_____ngkuh_____li_____ttuh_____lstah_____

Consonants that are capable of sustaining pitch, such as n, m, l, and ng can sometimes get in the way at this stage. Other consonants such as p, k, and t, will just foreshorten the previous word and chop up the phrase.

So we should have

Twi_____ngkuh_____ltwi_____ngkuh_____l

not

Twing_____kuhl_____twing_____kuhl_____

Speak the words of various nursery rhymes or short poems to practise this. The vibration in the chest should feel almost completely constant.

Combining the notes with the speaking element

Notes + Words = Singing

Using both hands at the same time.

The easiest way to describe this is that one hand does the speaking element action while the other does the moving note action. At first, this is a bit like patting your head while you are rubbing your tummy (or in this case, chest), but this should quickly become easier.

You are now multi-tasking! Actually conscious multi-tasking does not really exist. The brain and body quickly flit from one task to the next. Therefore let the mind flit from the sensation of speaking to the sensation of vibrating, moving notes in the head. Practise this activity until it really feels like you are doing nothing more than these two individual tasks simultaneously.

When you are experiencing these sensations, what emerges is more than the sum of the two parts. The breath is now connected to the speaking element, while the note is being moved by a thought. In our opinion, this concept is fundamental to gaining vocal freedom in singing.

Hum a note, a vibration somewhere above the roof of the mouth and then speak a word, 'one' or 'two' or any other word in your home area, as previously discussed. Put one hand on your head and the other on your chest to remind you of the sensations worked on earlier. Alternate between humming the note and speaking the word. Maintain the sensation of each separately. Do this four or five times, and then take a leap of faith and perform both of these two sensations simultaneously.

Repeat this exercise on various pitches and different words. You may now be able to feel these two elements simultaneously. When this happens, continue to use this short exercise until this feeling becomes more natural.

Next, take two pitches close together and try combining with a single word in the same way. Instruct yourself to speak regardless of the movement of the notes. Extend this idea to three notes and onwards to your song melodies. The speaking element should remain a sustained vibration throughout.

Vowels

In all singing methods, much is spoken about vowels. They are often deconstructed in a technical way to help a student create a particular musical style or a particular tonal palette suitable for a style of singing, such as Opera or contemporary American Musical Theatre. For example, operatic basses tend to gravitate to the darker spectrum of vowel sounds while light sopranos will tend to the brighter. This approach is somewhat simplistic, because character choices and psychological influences, as well as the repertoire and genre in which the singer is singing should all be having an effect on the vowel shapes.

The acoustic properties of vowel shapes are such that bright tone to dark tone is promoted from the Italian i (as in *i*nfamy) through e (t*e*rror), a (tr*a*gedy), o (h*o*rror), to u (r*u*in). The English words which we use to illustrate are to be pronounced in RP or Received Pronunciation (the standard accent learned by

British actors), as to go into phonetics may be complicated for this purpose. Whispering these sounds might give you an idea of this concept as you tune into a rise and fall in pitch.

Particular tendency towards one singing colour is not what we are aiming for. Rather we look for a range of colour – the bel canto school called this chiaroscuro (light/dark). Adjustments in the habitual use of vowels can be a good remedial tool to provide balance for voices that have become physically stuck in one tonal palette, be it overly bright or dark.

We usually explore Italian vowels with our students in order to take them on what is often a particularly interesting journey. This may be because of the physicality that these vowels elicit, or it may be that these vowels are somehow more connected to exclamatory tone when they are explored in their pure form. Furthermore, we believe that the earliest bel canto ideals of the Florentine Camerata would not have led to such momentous outcomes if the concepts that they were exploring were not interacting with the inherent qualities in the Italian language itself.

We are of course well aware that language – indeed human expression itself – demands an almost infinite spectrum of shapes and colours for vowel sounds, however we see these particular Italian vowels as being the primary colours in our exploration of free expressive singing.

So, quite early on in a student's training, we work on old Italian songs or Arie Antiche. This is not because of our classical training or simply repertoire that we feel comfortable with. These songs demand a long flowing vocal line and allow you to inhabit these pure vowels that not only form the poetry but also the expression itself. Therefore, in this repertoire, it is as if the song itself is teaching you to sing. Moreover the extent to which you fulfil the song's needs is directly related to what you gain from singing it.

Ramon Vargas – 'Amarilli Mia Bella' by Caccini
In this orchestrated version, Vargas demonstrates beautiful balanced resonance, superb legato line and a tone quality of fully bright and fully dark. His full tone always seems capable of a *diminuendo*, which is a true sign of vocal freedom.

Singing does not sound like ordinary speaking. We expect the best type of singing in the theatre to be transformed tonally from this ordinary sound world to communicate feelings that can fully encompass human experience.

Sarah Connolly – 'Dido's Lament' from *Dido and Aeneas* by Henry Purcell and Nahum Tate – BBC Proms, 2009
One of our leading contemporary mezzo sopranos singing perhaps the most famous aria from early English opera. The recitative in this piece is slowed down to facilitate greater expression and the aria is built on a repeating descending bass motif. Connolly's singing exemplifies bel canto in its legato, balance and expression and is never musically or theatrically indulgent to the detriment of authenticity. Stunning live singing.

In Musical Theatre in particular, many songs might start with a sound that is related to the character's spoken quality or dialect but if this remains fixed as the song progresses, we are quite often left with a feeling of disappointment. This is because the depth of expression indicated in the song is not connected in a finely detailed way to the actor's body. A good actor/singer will always make the appropriate transition.

Barbra Streisand – 'Where Is It Written' from *Yentl* by Michel Legrand and Alan and Marilyn Bergman – film soundtrack 1983

Streisand's voice is unmistakable. We can hear a speech quality in her communication. Her legato in this song is very pure; her ability to sing long flowing lines her hallmark. She demonstrates a belt mix technique in this excerpt (see Miscellany for belt voice and mixed voice) and her voice is always balanced to express her feelings in musical as well as theatrical terms. Her tone never becomes shouty when exploring more passionate expression.

Exploring Italian vowels

Nicolai Gedda – 'Vocalise' by Rachmaninov – 1970 EMI recording with Alexis Weissenberg (piano)

The Swedish tenor Nicolai Gedda demonstrates an incredible example of how to sing a pure Italian 'a' vowel. This requires superb concentration and a feel for vocal freedom. Gedda's control of dynamics is unsurpassed and he sings a perfect mezza voce (from the Italian meaning 'half voice') with no change in core colour. His rising phrase at the end to D flat shows his mixed voice quality and is not falsetto. Gedda's musicality is astonishing and he seems at one with Rachmaninov. This heartfelt expression without words is a superb example of how the voice can be thought of as a musical instrument, indeed perhaps the most expressive and immediate of all musical instruments. If you are inspired by Gedda, look up his recordings of 'Lenski's aria' from Tchaikovsky's opera *Eugene Onegin*, and the song 'Les Eaux du Printemps' by Rachmaninov.

Working with notes in your lower and middle pitch range, place the tip of your forefinger in your mouth – as if pointing to the back of the mouth – with your teeth lightly resting above and below your finger. This is approximately the correct spacing of the jaw for all of these Italianate vowels:

- a (as in tr**a**gedy)
- e (as in t**e**rror)

- i (as in *i*nfamy)
- o (as in h**o**rror)
- u (as in r**u**in)

It is most important that you do not attempt to put anything between your teeth that can be swallowed or get stuck in your throat! For example, an object such as a cork should never be placed between the teeth when singing exercises.

You may be surprised by how small the required amount of space is between the teeth, which also relates to the position of the jaw, but you may feel that this promotes a good feeling for freedom and flexibility in the throat. Often consciously limiting the space at the front of the mouth leads to a better feeling for space further back. This is what we call 'closed open' singing and is a stepping stone to 'open open' singing which involves the same feeling in the throat but a free use of the jaw (not a conscious opening). Actors need this freedom in the moment to express their character and to play their action. Be aware in this exercise of the movement of your lips for the different vowels, bringing to life the exclamatory nature of the word indicated: tragedy, terror, and so forth. Allow the lips to move a little more actively than may be habitual in normal speech.

Articulation

Articulation, which is the movement of the tongue, lips, jaw and so forth, to form words, needs to be particularly flexible for actors who usually rely less on tonal stylistic aesthetics and more on truthful storytelling and characterisation.

Words should be articulated in song as in well-produced speech. They should not be coloured consciously in an effort to spit the words out or make them more special. This is a function of the imagination. We often work on a student's articulation in speech as well as in song and are fortunate at RADA to be able to refer our students to some of the finest experts in their field. When the voice has been well conditioned and vocal support developed, the words will be carried naturally on the controlled stream of breath that is necessary for good singing.

Beginners often exhibit a 'fight or flight' response to articulation in singing, either producing an inhibited, under-energized response, or, in an attempt to be clearer, using too much air pressure, which has a knock-on effect, preventing the release of natural and balanced vocal tone. Actors and student actors alike will usually be well versed in articulation exercises. Tongue-twisters can be helpful.

- Open your mouth a little.
- Flick your tongue up and down as in the consonant 'l' without moving the jaw or using any sound and then simultaneously start to sing a sustained Italian 'a' vowel (as in tragedy) on any note.

  You will automatically get la, la, la.

  This consonant is purely a movement of the tongue and there should be no movement of the jaw.
- Place a hand lightly underneath your chin to encourage the stillness of your jaw.

- Now do the same with the consonant 'm', this time using your lips. Be aware of how little movement you need in the jaw to accomplish this.

- Simultaneously start to sing an Italian 'u' vowel (as in r*u*in). You will similarly get mu, mu, mu.

Using a simple song as a study

In song singing we are putting together all the various elements that we have been looking at in isolation, or in various combinations.

As with relearning any skill that you want to improve, you will undoubtedly slip into habitual usage in certain elements while focusing your attention on some new elements. Perhaps in the beginning in moving the note upwards in the head you lose the sensation of the spoken element or by focusing on these two things you find you have lost your optimum state of posture. Ultimately what will happen with repetition is that more of the elements will be incorporated into the whole in their optimum state.

Putting it all Together

Take 'Twinkle Twinkle Little Star' as an example.

- Think about your posture, the attitude of the sternum, the back lengthening and widening, the neck being free. Your weight should be equally distributed. Blow the candle as if to gently disturb its flame.

- Remember that the in breath is a reflex and does not affect the attitude of the posture.

- Head hum the melody in a pitch range that feels comfortable. Be aware of how this feels. Place a hand on your head to help with this sensation of movement. Sense the lift box sensation.

- Speak the words smoothly (legato) in a declamatory style in your home area in the rhythm of the song. Be aware of the feel of vibration in the chest.

- Sing the notes smoothly on a pure Italian vowel of your choice, maintaining the space between your teeth (again you might use your forefinger as a guide) to experience the 'closed open' sensation explored earlier.

- Repeat this, approximating the words of the song but taking away the articulation of the consonants. These sounds should be sustained and perfectly legato. You will now be aware of the internal movements as you sing the melody with the vowels of the song

- Whisper the words of your song, focusing on the amount of movement needed to articulate them with precision and intention.

- Put all these together!

Take the example of riding a bike. When you take cycling seriously you may need to relearn how to ride your bike with a renewed technique and have to unlearn old habits – you still have to keep upright, but not make that your main focus. Likewise, this is a new sort of singing, and one which to coordinate naturally will need a lot of practice. Let your coordination develop in your own time. You may have some fun with this exercise as you become more and more aware of the freedom that you are finding and become more eager to practise. This may seem a mechanical way to start, but remember: the postural and breathing elements should feel natural and fundamental, the speaking element allows you not to push or lift the word and will in time be owned by your intention, while the notes should be a sensation in your head and free from tension.

Despite its seeming simplicity, this worthwhile coordination exercise may produce a profound effect. If you have the opportunity, it can be useful to use a full-length mirror periodically to check that the head and neck are not making any extraneous movements and that the sternum is not collapsing as the phrases progress.

We often choose to use nursery rhymes to introduce this exercise, as we did not think to question ourselves when we first sang them and also because students usually know them already. Their lack of any particular tonal expectations or obvious emotionality is also useful, because both of these elements can be distracting at this stage. These will be introduced later in the process on other material, once your technique is up and running.

These exercises and experiments with various nursery rhymes should continue for a few weeks. The aim is efficiency and coordination.

Having sung several nursery rhymes, move on to sing one or two folk songs or maybe Shakespeare songs. Use songs that are not too wide-ranging in pitch, and where the tune sits in an area of the voice that feels comfortable for you.

Initially, when working on your technique, it may be beneficial to practise in small, concentrated amounts. In time, the body and brain will habituate to the correct sensations, to be remembered and experienced again later or tomorrow and eventually the sensations of these components will merge towards one sensation, that of free voice.

Progress may come steadily, but it is not uncommon for there to be a sudden penny-dropping moment. Sometimes the determination to do something can be the extra catalyst needed. Luciano Pavarotti set a deadline, and challenged himself to have achieved a certain level of success or give up the idea of a career in singing. The rest is history!

The authors have two anecdotes to offer:

'I was learning to swim, and one day I almost managed to do it. I went home and thought through all the elements and told myself I would be able to swim the next time I went. I convinced my mother that I should go back to the pool the next day and sure enough I could swim!'

'When I was a student, I was laid low with a virus for a few weeks and during that time, out of boredom more than anything else, managed in complete silence to imagine and sense the experience of bringing into balance simultaneously all the components of singing. When I was better, sure enough, everything came together. I seemed to have trained my brain to assimilate all of the tasks into one physicality, and I never looked back.'

Constructing a technical process is like this at the start – 'spinning plates', as we sometimes describe it. You focus on one plate and as soon as that one is properly spinning, another one has practically crashed and you need to focus on that one, and so forth. Eventually, with practice, you will become more able to keep all the plates spinning at more or less the same rate. But it will always require awareness.

Another image is one of learning to drive. All of the separate functions need to be practised separately – the pedals, the gears and the steering – until they become totally coordinated and you can do all of them automatically while listening to your favourite comedy programme on the car radio. You go through different stages of proficiency before you become an advanced driver.

Registers, Bridges and Passages (Passaggi)

You may be waiting with bated breath to see what we have to say on the subject of the 'break', which is a major concern of many singers. Let us tell you that there are no tricks here! Talking about a break in the voice is not constructive and so we prefer to focus our work on the areas of the voice referred to as the bridges or passages (passaggi).

> 'No man or woman can sing the wrong register without holding rigidly the instrument they sing with. A singer is one whose whole instrument should show litheness throughout' – William Shakespeare (the singing teacher)

We can assume that if you are singing flexibly and without any tension, the mechanics of your voice will adjust naturally for whichever register you are singing in. Sound and pitch are simply vibrations, and the different sorts of vibrations in the vocal folds denote the registers in the voice.

Interestingly, the Florentine Camerata based some of their musical theory on the concept of the particular powers of the low, intermediate and high regions or registers of the voice, which they felt were 'capable of moving listeners to various moral persuasions'!

Vocal bridges are the areas of the voice where you move from one register to another. A register is a series of notes that have a similar vocal timbre. As you sing upwards through your range, you may notice a change in quality. This may also be the case as you sing downward through your vocal range. Registers have in the past and even to this day been referred to as head and chest, but should also include middle. The terms 'head voice' and 'chest voice' are not to be confused with head and chest register. These terms can be especially misleading as a concept for the female voice, as these are more of a descriptor of a voice that has not found a natural balance of resonance due to inappropriate tensions or undeveloped technique.

The key to developing an even tone throughout the voice in order to bridge the registers is to concentrate on maintaining the feeling of a naturalized speaking element while balancing this with the sensation of the notes as discussed earlier. The pay-off, when this is successfully managed, is quite often a more balanced and expressive middle and top register. This process requires a good deal of concentration, application and patience.

Every singer and singing teacher may have a different strategy for how to deal with bridges, but we feel that the key lies in the general condition of your vocal instrument. The bigger the instrument, the bigger the potential breaks, so a bigger voice generally needs more conditioning, and perhaps more time to fully develop.

In natural human expression, as we get more agitated, pitch will rise and tension seems more apparent. Perhaps because of inherent tension, the areas of the voice around the bridges, especially the upper bridge, often carry a great deal of emotional expression in music.

The singer and teacher Jean de Reszke particularly mentions the upper of the two vocal bridges when speaking about expression and proposes that expressiveness in singing comes from the middle register and from the bridge notes to the high register. Later in this chapter we have included exercises which use playfulness to engage the voice in different ways, thereby easing inherent tensions through a flexible approach.

You may feel a build-up of tension as you sing upwards from your lower register, and doing exercises that go downwards through the voice may be helpful. In some voices, noticing how you manage the balance of the resonances on the way down may be helpful in managing them better on the way up. Sometimes exploring singing through these areas on an 'ng' sound can be helpful. If the principles of combining the speaking element and the note are adhered to, the middle register of the voice should feel balanced, authentic and capable of easy expression. Working downwards from the middle, more chest resonance naturally comes into play and it may be in danger of 'breaking' after you have descended a few notes. Care must be taken at certain pitches to keep the notes balanced with the words. It sometimes helps to be more aware of the note sensation as you descend and the word sensation as you ascend. This balance can be adjusted by experimentation to manage these different areas more skilfully. Alternatively some students find that to lighten the voice under the passaggi works well for them. With men's voices, one possibility in the upper passage is to 'break' into falsetto.

The fundamental principles of breathing and posture are of paramount importance here. One of the reasons why singers have problems in these areas is because they change the breath pattern or alter their posture in some way, even if it is very slight. For example, the chin might poke forwards so the neck is shortened, or you forget to keep the breath 'speaking' the word.

A homogenous sound as a basis is very important in singing – so we have to find a way to achieve this, otherwise the voice may exhibit a heady or hooty sound when moving upward through the passaggi. This is only one example, but using a vocal trick to deal with the bridge is undesirable and can make you sound like two different people!

The middle register is where the actor/singer reveals their true colours. If you 'cover' (deliberately alter the vowel shape) in the middle register, this might lead to a loss of truth, authenticity and personality in the voice. The covered sound often sounds louder in the singer's head, but it loses tonal balance and complexity.

The passaggi can be a major concern in classical singing where evenness of tone and a large range are paramount. In order to manage the passaggi, a voice needs flexibility and support and the actor should continue to work around these areas in exercises and to sing while being sensitive and aware of the balance in the sound.

Every voice has different issues regarding passaggi or bridges. We work on an individual basis to solve these and do not aim to erase vocal bridges, but to enable you to negotiate them with greater ease. It is outside the realms of a book to offer solutions to every student regarding difficulties with bridges, although they will become less of an obstacle in your work as you achieve the vocal balance that so many of the exercises in this book seek to establish. These areas are the most vulnerable in the voice and, when mastered, are the key to real expertise and supreme proficiency.

Support

Support is an extremely important facet of good singing. A well-supported voice is one in which the physical, vocal and psychological gestures that together form an actor's dramatic expression are perfectly matched in accordance with nature. Support is sometimes referred to as being centred on the diaphragm. However, this is an area where singers can hold much personal tension and this tension often disrupts the body's natural ability to contract and relax in this area, throwing the whole system out of balance. When this is evident, we work more holistically to restore the balance and we tend not to look for a cure by instructing the diaphragm itself. Paradoxically it is often the case that the instruction to soften the body in the abdominal and diaphragm area, together with a greater need to express your thoughts and emotions, produces a more accurate muscular action in the abdomen and back, and a more appropriate supported tone.

There is much misunderstanding around the subject of support and students often search for 'the answer', or a fixed way in which they can support their voice. In our opinion, support is not entirely physical. Rather, it is the natural physical condition when the body is functioning in a heightened state, and as such is also a function of theatrical and physical awareness. When working on support we often use the instruction to play an action in a heightened state, while maintaining good posture and breathing. We also work in this manner on songs to further explore its physical manifestation.

The feeling of support is intrinsically connected with the in breath, the posture, the status of the mind and body, and crucially with the operation of the larynx which holds the air back to create vocal tone. A good way to sense the feeling of support is to use the Alexander Technique principle of lengthening and widening, when singing. The in breath should not ever be so big as to feel that the ribcage no longer has the potential to widen further. When singing, the mind can give the instruction to the ribcage to feel like it is ever widening, and not locked in one position. The onset of the sound is very often where a collapse or lock occurs in the ribcage, and the feeling of support can promote better phonation (the act of turning breath into sound) in many students.

Ultimately good support is a very muscular action, and teachers help its acquisition by giving you songs which very gradually increase your range, both in pitch and in the length of phrases and dramatic content. A teacher turning down your choice of song as being 'too big for you' means just that – that the demands of the song outweigh your physical and mental ability to keep the voice at the centre healthy at that stage in your progress. Without the help of a good teacher it is difficult to differentiate between tension and correct use of the supporting muscles. Over time the supporting muscles grow in strength and flexibility.

Musical Exercises

Here are some musical exercises to get your voice moving. You can build sequences for yourself, but the following are typical progressions. It is a good idea to become proficient at finding notes on a musical keyboard. You can download an app onto your mobile phone or tablet, or possibly buy a small portable music keyboard – often found in toy shops. Confidence in using a keyboard will help with working out awkward corners in songs later on as well. While advanced musical knowledge is always helpful, it is not needed initially. Many keyboard apps follow a numbering system, which helps you to find the exact pitches that you are looking for.

There are also some apps which will play warm-up exercises to suit the amount of time you have and your vocal range. Any simple exercise will do – it's not what you do, it's the way that you do it!

Once you have a few standard exercises up your sleeve, you no longer need to listen to them, just give yourself a starting note and proceed – moving that starting point up or down in semitones (the smallest step between any two keys on a piano keyboard).

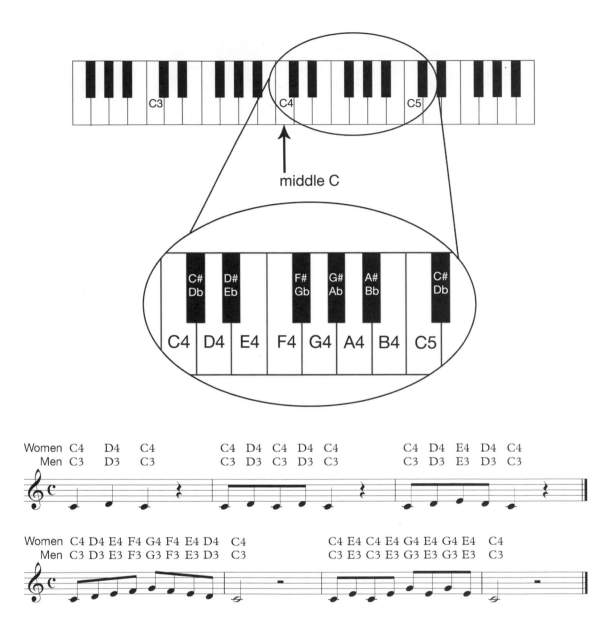

Begin with just one vowel on these simple exercises and over a period of days and weeks, use a variety of starting notes and different vowels and you will end up with a set of exercises that probably will not be too dissimilar to the scales and arpeggios that you may have heard already.

Through correct and repetitive functioning, your aim should be to do all of the above exercises fairly consistently, with an awareness of the basic principles as you are singing them.

Once you have worked through these basic exercises, moving elegantly between the notes and seeking to maintain all the basic good practices of posture and breathing, you should build up a whole series of exercises, examples of which are given on the following pages.

Women start on C4
Men start on C3

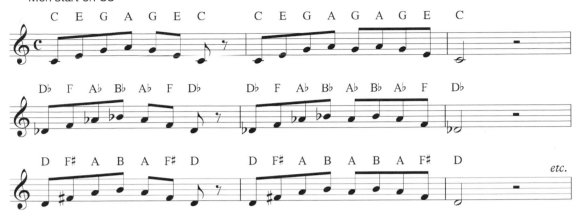

Women start on B flat 4
Men start on B flat 3

Women start on A4
Men start on A3

Then try a whole set of broken chords (or arpeggios):

Women start on B flat 3
Men start on B flat 2

The next set of exercises might go like this – descending arpeggios:

Women start on B flat 4
  Men start on B flat 3

Also descending scales:

Women start on B flat 4
  Men start on B flat 3

Then add in some consonants on a repeated arpeggio:

Women start on B flat 3
  Men start on B flat 2

Next,
u – lu, i – li etc.

Then try other combinations of consonants and vowels. The movement of the consonant should not feel as though it affects the flow of the vowels.

For example, with 'l' it is just a flick of the tongue.

Next – try staccato, in combination with the smooth legato line that you have already been using. Staccato feels like a giggle – short and detached.

In the following exercise, the first group of four notes (which are marked with a slur) are to be sung legato and the second group of four (with the dot below the note) staccato.

Women start on B flat 3
  Men start on B flat 2

This may look a bit complex, but allowing a little time to get to grips with the logic behind the keyboard will not only help you learn the basic exercises that you will come across in many singing vocal warm-ups, but also puts you in control of finding notes for yourself.

If you can find your way around a computer keyboard, there is no reason why, with practice, you cannot do the same on a musical one. Put your keyboard on a surface at waist height. The worst thing you can do is to hunch over a keyboard to give yourself a note, as all your posture work will fly out the window.

At the beginning of training it is important to work mainly in the middle of your voice, but you should make sure that you work outwards from the middle towards the extremes of your pitch range every day. If you do this, you should find that gradually your range extends over time.

A basic knowledge of music theory and basic piano keyboard skills will help you greatly and should be seen as an investment. We include these components in the Foundation Course at RADA as we believe they are tools that actors need. Patterns of notes can be useful tools to take you through your whole range. Later on it can also work well to use random phrases from songs to practise the techniques you have learned so far.

Further Exercises

The following are ideas which have been explored with students for general conditioning and to help them overcome specific difficulties. They can be thought of as tonics which explore various elements involved in singing on stage. We are fully aware that words cannot completely describe their application, and that in working with a student, the exercises might evolve as they go along.

Some of these exercises, specifically the ones that have an auditory element involved, may be more useful to work on with a singing teacher. All are here to promote mental, physical and vocal flexibility as part of the process of conditioning your instrument. The following exercises do not deconstruct singing in a conventional way but we think their nature is none the less technical for it. Technique as we see it is a means to an end.

'When a key is offered for use, I am not among those who are turning it over and over unable to decide from the look of it whether it is good metal or base metal. The question for me is whether it will unlock the door' – Arthur Eddington, astrophysicist

Joel Gray – 'If You Could See Her Through My Eyes' from *Cabaret* by Kander and Ebb – Film, 1972
Joel Gray's technique is impeccable, revealing a light lyric tenor of considerable ease which allows him the freedom to play as he wishes with the text and the melody. Iconic and inspiring.

Balance ball

This is an exercise which addresses issues in the imbalance of head and chest resonance, or the note and speaking quality as we have described it. It might be that the voice sounds too *heady* or *hooty* or that it is overly heavy or harsh. We are after a mix and a sensation of balanced tone in the middle register. This exercise is also helpful in negotiating vocal bridges. The physicality in this exercise might be a useful learning tool for visual learners, while it also promotes kinaesthetic awareness.

Imagine you have a globe the size of a football (soccer ball). Hold it out in front of you with your hands covering its north and south poles. The top hand represents head resonance (head humming quality) and the bottom hand, chest resonance (speech quality). Extend one of your hands away from the body around the globe to add that particular quality to your speech and song and towards the body to have less of that quality. In other words, the top hand on the north pole moves away from you to explore more head hum as the lower hand on the south pole moves towards you for less speech quality, or vice versa. Explore your sound when adding extra chest or head resonance. A teacher might help you achieve an appropriate balance which might seem at first to be not natural for you. This is an instance when you really need to rely on a trustworthy and experienced ear to guide you. You can employ this exercise when singing one note or can extend it to three-note or five-note exercises or passages from your songs.

Shouting or pushing in either speech or song can cause vocal strain, and in this exercise would in fact produce a prominent attack from the bottom hand.

The calling position and the open throat

This explores an element of the vocal transformation needed for singing on stage. This works well for a voice lacking vitality and projection and for a throat that is habitually closed or under-energized.

Place cupped hands to the mouth and, with good posture, tilt the head up a little, as if calling up from an imaginary cartoon hole in the ground. Yes, you can move your head, as good posture does not

Kelly Burke in *Poppy* by Monty Norman and Peter Nichols: RADA Production 2008. Photographer: Mick Hurdus

necessitate one obvious physical position! (This upward tilt of the head is a means to an end and not an aesthetic choice for singing.) Invent some text such as: 'Hello up there, I've fallen down a big hole in the ground and broken my leg! Could you go and get some help?' Have some fun with calling out the text and avoid an overtly emotional or realistic vocalisation which can confuse the issue that this exercise is intended to address. Explore different pitch ranges and avoid a pushed or shouted tone.

When a good, free, calling tone is made, you can sustain some of the text and even develop it into musical patterns to connect this feel for tone to musical pitches. Refer to the musical exercises illustrated earlier. When you get a good feel for this, repeat this with the head in a more neutral position.

This exercise promotes a natural 'open throat' as well as greater mental and physical engagement in the act of phonation. Exploring a calling and not a sung tone can reduce expectation and fear in certain students, as calling tone is seldom judged whereas sung tone certainly can be by the new student.

Focusing on the pitch function

Take a piece of text such as the 'Carmen Vocis' in our 'Prelude' or maybe the text of a song. Speak the text in the voice that you would use when introducing a concert or telling a story on stage. Certain students may adopt a vocal tone that has a quality of pretence; this is not desirable and these tensions must not be developed, however the way we speak on stage is not the same as our everyday voice.

Speak the words in a limited pitch range about a third higher than the deepest note in your voice – four or five small steps (semitones) on the keyboard. This is approximately your home area in terms of pitch, that is to say, where you are not lifting or pushing down in any way.

Now start to make the tune of your speech a little more sing-songy. The instruction is to do no more work. Extend the pitch range to transform the limited but natural spoken inflection into something even more sing-songy. There should be no conscious muscular effort in this transformation. Avoid any conscious transformation to sung tone.

Listen to your new tune emerging from the text and repeat it to ma ma ma, mi mi mi, mu mu mu and so forth. Still the instruction is to do no more work or create no more tension when doing this. Focus on maintaining the same tune elicited by your spoken inflection. As always, maintain good posture.

When this can be done successfully, repeat this emerging 'tune' on one vowel – the Italian vowels (a, e, i, o, u) will work well in this exercise. Make sure that you focus on the sustaining of the vowel and avoid any feeling of acceleration or deceleration of the breath as you ascend or descend in pitch. Some students, who habitually increase or decrease air pressure under the larynx to pitch (often referred to as pushing or devoicing), might get the sensation of stillness in the breath as the pitch moves.

Remember, the breath speaks the word, the thought moves the note. Focus on the task. Keep speaking and communicating. If you find yourself judging how you are doing by 'listening in', you are not focusing enough on the task and you will not be in the moment.

Drinking in your sound

This exercise explores the idea that vocal onset (or the launch of a tone) can be felt as an implosion as well as an explosion. This sensation is particularly apparent when starting a note on a vowel and not a consonant. The old Italians spoke of 'inhalare la voce' (inhale the voice) as a sensation that should be developed to benefit expression in singing.

We will be using imagery and relaxation techniques to explore this concept and also to address habitual glottal attack and general tension caused by anxiety in the launch or start of a note, particularly on a vowel. Glottal attack is explained on page 130 in the chapter on Troubleshooting.

For the purpose of this exercise we will assume that a vibration can be started in the head just with the power of thought. So, think of the expression of agreement: 'mm–hmm'. Do not listen to yourself but focus on being truthful. Now sustain the first hummed sound. Imagine that this sound is a vibration somewhere in the head. Now sing an open Italian vowel by sending this vibration down and out of the mouth. Now explore the sensation of sending the vibrated sound down into the body. It may help to momentarily tilt the head back a little to help the sensation of inhaling or drinking in the vibration. Nasality should not occur if your hum has been correctly initiated. Ensure a clean attack by thinking of the drinking sensation the instant the vibration occurs.

If the body remains tense at the onset of tone, then sitting down can be helpful for certain students and giving the instruction to remain passive or soft in the abdominal area. This can help the feeling of diaphragmatic support as opposed to abdominal grip.

The flexible throat and free jaw

Continuing from the exercise above, this exercise places the focus on the sensation of movement in the vocal tract centring on the soft palate. This is a good exercise to explore the reflex action of the soft palate.

Place the tip of your index finger gently between the teeth, and repeat the exercise above to produce a sustained sound on an Italian 'a'. Now move the pitch a tone or a minor third (two or three small steps on the keyboard). If the interval (the distance between the notes) is sung without a slide, then some movement may be detected at the back of the throat. Direct the throat to remain relaxed in this exercise; do not be actively involved in this area of the body but merely aware of any movement in it. You may notice that a lift can be sensed when moving to a higher note. Extend this feeling to musical patterns and onwards to any tune pattern including song melodies and, for the more advanced, the vocal trill or oscillation. The relaxed stillness draws attention to the flexible inner workings of the vocal mechanism.

To sing as we speak

This is another concept passed down from the early Italians. We believe this refers to a sensation within the singer and does not at all refer to a tonal aesthetic. Singing should not for the most part sound like speech and, furthermore, we could say that singing starts when speaking is not enough for our expressive needs. In this exercise, musical and theatrical demands are treated equally and the note is equal to the word.

Over-articulation can often be the cause of tension, preventing the nuanced adjustment necessary in the throat for free vocal tone, especially when singing in the middle and upper registers. This is sometimes heard in choral singers who have the majority of their energy seemingly centred on the lips, jaw and tongue. If the voice is properly 'centred' then there should not be any need to spit the words out in order to be heard or understood.

Whisper the words of your song with the fingers of one hand lightly placed on your lips. Sense the ease of movement of the lips, jaw and tongue and the natural fall of the jaw that you need to express clarity of thought. Repeat these movements when adding your melody. Alternate between the whisper and the sung phrase and when adding the note, feel that there is no need to compromise what you previously discovered. Be aware of any change in tone that this might elicit, but concentrate on this new feeling and allow the sound that emerges from it to be in the moment and not pre-empted in any way. Posture is important, and be certain to maintain an appropriate connection with your speaking element.

We often find it useful to instruct students, when exploring notes in the upper middle and top register, to momentarily play with the idea of being an overindulgent opera singer whose words play second fiddle to the glory of their tone. This may in some cases allow the necessary adjustment in the vowel to enable the student to access the upper notes with greater ease. It is often surprising how a student discovers the quite natural mechanism of vowel modification by this means, although ultimately, operatic tone is not necessarily the desired aesthetic.

Relaxation and supporting in the moment

Students can often be confused when working on a particular vocal problem by one teacher urging them to *support* where another has told them that they should *relax*. The truth is that these seemingly opposite solutions may amount to the same thing.

F. M. Alexander hypothesized that correct muscular involvement with voice could be discovered by a system known as inhibition (saying 'no' to unnecessary habitual tension).

Posture is of paramount importance as always. Instruct the abdominal area to soften as you call out 'hey you!' and maybe 'hello there!'. Continue to instruct passivity in this area (say 'no' to active muscular involvement) but let your mind be aware of the action of the diaphragm and abdominal area. Even when attempting to be completely soft and passive in this area, this may be felt as an impossibility on the onset of this vigorous vocalisation. Nevertheless, continual instruction to relax while focusing on this area will encourage specific awareness of correct support as opposed to non-specific abdominal tension. The more delicate the vocal onset, the more advanced the exercise becomes as the sensation of support becomes less evident. More kinaesthetically aware students may be able to feel the engagement of the support in even a delicate onset. Extend this exercise by working with various Italian vowels.

Fearless sostenuto

It may be that you have developed a habit of stabilising your singing tone to benefit musical needs such as steadiness of pitch, equality of volume between notes, a wide range, but this may have been to the detriment of your authenticity and clarity of intention. In this case the following exercise might be a step towards redressing the balance. This exercise suggests not sustaining at all!

Speed the song up and do not attempt to sustain any of the words. Stay on the pitches of the song and sing with energy and conviction. Now imagine a slow-motion version of your speeded-up singing. This might give you greater freedom in your attack or a different feel for singing. Alternate between fast non-sustained singing and singing with the appropriate tempo and rhythm. Many actors enjoy this exercise, as anything that helps diminish fear or tension seems also to promote imagination and enjoyment.

Connecting to space: Dynamic singing

Flick your fingers with each syllable of the words as you speak the lyrics of the song. Use both hands.

Place your hands just in front of you at the level of your breast bone and let the direction of the flicking be gently upwards. Now aim the flicking directly at the imaginary (or real) person that you are speaking to in your song. Let your arms reach out more. Now aim the flicking up and out to the 'gods'. Extend your arms.

Observe how the pitch range, resonance and dynamics are changed by this exercise. These changes are induced by the imagination, and a student who does not exhibit any changes of expression in the speaking voice when doing this exercise should be encouraged to land their thought on the desired party with renewed intention and desire!

Now repeat the exercise when singing the lyrics. Do not predetermine how you are going to use this physicality when you employ it for the first time in your song, just go with your impulse. You might want to try your song several times before coming to any conclusions. Do not attempt to control the vocal dynamic but let the voice respond to the physicality induced by the flicking.

Timing and attack

Another exercise that works by associating with physical ease and is both kinaesthetic and visual in its content.

Touch the wall lightly with the fingertips on the onset of a word or a moving pitch. Sing an arpeggio and touch higher spots on the wall when the pitch ascends (and lower when it descends). Explore what happens when the space between the spots on the wall is made smaller even when the movements in pitch remain the same.

Extend the exercise by touching an imaginary wall or the air in front of you instead. Feel any vocal changes and maintain these sensations when editing out the hand movements. Vocal glissandi or slides can also be worked on in this manner by sliding your fingertips up and down.

I stop, you start

In this exercise, the student and the teacher share the decision-making. We are exploring how the body adjusts according to its needs in order to express the next thought. This can inform crucial internal adjustments and particularly influence the critical moment just before the launch of the tone. It explores singing in the moment.

The teacher is in charge of stopping the song whenever he or she wants to, by saying 'stop'. This can be at the end of a phrase, before the beginning of a phrase – in fact, anywhere he or she wishes to do so. The student is in charge of continuing the song from where it stopped. The all-important instruction is to continue only when you are 'ready'. This can be any length of time.

After this has been explored and any interesting observations made, the exercise is done again, but this time the student must condense the time taken to 'get ready'. Continue to condense on further repetition or repetitions until the same state of readiness can be felt, but the song is returned to its musical and rhythmical boundaries. This works on many aspects of singing, both technical and artistic. In singing there is always a momentary pause between the in breath and phonation to set up the physical conditions for expression. This exercise explores that moment by allowing the student to take ownership of it, gaining impetus from the rhythm of the song and the inherent tonal expression.

Exclamatory tone: Valerio and Vittoria

These two Italian pizza chefs can form a great exercise!

For the student who loves to play, this can be highly creative and can elicit effortlessness by exploring high-energy physicality and tonal vitality while not creating unnecessary air pressure under the larynx (vocal pushing).

Play with a 'hide and seek' energy: 'Valerio! Where are you?' You can have some fun if there are any cupboards or trunks in the room by creeping up: 'Valerio! I know you're in there!' The tune can be playful and quite sing-songy. Look around the side of the piano to see if he might be there! Imagine that you are calling upstairs, or that you are getting cross that you cannot find him. Perhaps you are getting worried and frightened that he might have disappeared!

Extend the scene into clowning and maybe explore the darker side of hide and seek, such as loneliness and desolation. Move from simple fun to emotive expression. Try to find Vittoria as well and maybe become a member of the Italian family with an appropriate Italian accent yourself. Use the space that you have, the more the better! Extend this by starting to sing in an improvised recitative-like way with the tone that is emerging from your 'hide and seek' energy. You can remember this feeling and some of these sensations can be taken into formal musical patterns such as descending scales and arpeggios. This exercise can help with the bridges between chest and middle registers and in extension to the head register.

Men and women can further explore the calling quality in their voices by starting this exercise on the following pitches, while women can also begin to experiment with belted tone.

Women start on F4

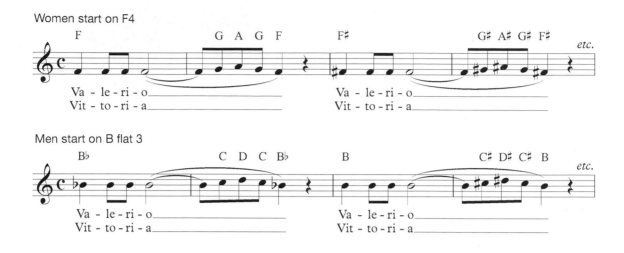

Men start on B flat 3

Conclusion

As you can see, we often use play and improvisation to place our actors firmly in their comfort zone, a conducive environment in which to encourage a free flow of the creative impulses which they have utilized alongside their singing technique from the outset. We are interested in finding ways of inducing spontaneous exclamatory tone and developing this sensation into truly authentic musical expression. We often move quite quickly from exercise to exercise in order to keep the process of discovery vital and creative, and we create new exercises which arise from the needs of individual students.

Using exercises that grow out of human impulses allows an actor the opportunity to offer an individual response, so that what we ultimately see and hear will be unique, based on their personal energy and approach.

Developing this individual response, based on a growing understanding of their own vocal instrument, gives our actors great confidence and is often the key component that makes their performances organic and compelling.

Singing taught me so much. It can be such a direct expression of emotion as it connects right to your gut. You are immediately connected to the word and its vibration. This was such a lesson for me. The training is essential as it helps you to understand your voice and how to control it. It stretches and exercises your voice, your throat, your breathing and your control and that can only help with speaking text and your performance of it. The discipline of singing taught me a lot about stamina and I doubt without that training I would have half the lung capacity I have now! The training and warm-up exercises I still use to this day. I was recently on stage in the West End – I wonder how my voice would have coped without my understanding of it and how to use it. So thank you for your wisdom and teaching! Singing training is invaluable to all.

Sally Hawkins – RADA graduate

9

THE ROLE OF THE COACH
AND THE ACCOMPANIST

The vocal coach, who is a pianist and perhaps an experienced musical director and conductor, will help you with the more musical and stylistic elements of the song, as opposed to the vocal and technical side of things.

The vocal coach serves many functions. They will:

- Teach you the notes in the first place.

- Suggest new repertoire as they get to know you and your voice, and propose repertoire for specific auditions.

- Check accuracy of pitches and rhythm.

- Help you understand how your melody fits with an accompaniment.

- Give advice on how a conductor may beat particular moments in the music and how the conductor can be there to help you.

- Tell you what to expect at auditions and provide you with an opportunity to create mock-audition situations.

- Help you to mark up songs for audition or performance, so that a new accompanist knows how you would like them played and which verses are being omitted. (It is a good idea to write breathing, tempo and dynamic markings into the music. It is wise to have two copies of your music, one for you and one for the accompanist, and always take a pencil and eraser to a coaching session.)

- Give guidance about good arrangements and accompaniments and advise you if any pieces are not suitable for audition due to the complexity of the accompaniment or the ensemble between the singer and the pianist. (Be warned that not all sheet music downloaded from the internet is musically accurate.)

- Advise on transposing songs into the correct key for your voice.

It may be that a coach can also suggest long-term projects. Perhaps they are involved in putting on cabarets, productions or concerts themselves and can encourage you to try some things out and start preparation. It may be that they encourage you to learn entire roles and work through entire musicals to work in more detail on style and characterisation, and to build stamina.

There are coaches who have specialist interests and skills and have more experience in certain genres. You should always go to a coach who gives you confidence to sing your song.

The very best coaches and accompanists will have great empathy and be able to respond to the performance of an actor as well as inspire it. Coaches will also be able to work with a singer on performance aspects of the material encompassing elements of style as well as content.

Both your teacher and your coach should have the ability to inspire artistic expression. It is an interesting conundrum to assess whether creating the physical and mental conditions for vocal freedom (the job of the teacher), or the intellectual understanding of the needs of the character and what compels that character to sing (the job of the coach), will create a more rounded artistic and profound expression. Good vocal coaching can certainly create the conditions for vocal freedom of expression and as such be regarded as giving technical improvement to the sound.

Likewise, a good teacher can inspire physical and vocal freedom in a completely different way which brings the poetry to life and creates a profound telling of the story of the song. The authors' belief is that a rounded training should include both of these crucial aspects and that it is the personality of each student that will ultimately dictate the modus operandi that will best develop them as singers.

There is a moment when you make the transition between being a student of a coach – where they are the one leading the process, and also perhaps controlling pace, rhythm, for example – to taking the reins a bit more yourself. It may be the case that many conductors wish to take the lead completely. However some conductors, and certainly accompanists, will ultimately expect you to take a lead, and when you gain in experience you need to find the confidence to put yourself more in control of the music-making. This involves listening and interacting with the accompanist. It is often achieved by literally breathing together, or certainly through 'feeling' the music as one.

Being able to lead a performance of a song is often one of the most important qualities that a musical director is likely to be looking for in an audition. If your accompanist in an audition feels that you are taking the lead, for example helping them with subtle cues by how you are breathing, and at what pace you lead into a phrase, this will be taken as a positive sign that you are in control of what you are doing. Then your accompanist can work alongside you. Remember that you and your accompanist are making music together. Your performance begins with the first note of music and you should be aware of what the piano plays before, during and after your song. You need to draw from and integrate this music, which may be expressing the character's feelings and thoughts, into your overall performance.

In complex music it is often the case that accompanists are playing in opposition to your melody, for example you are legato while the piano is staccato or vice versa, or that the 'character' of the piano playing or the emotional journey of the piano part is different from yours. Perhaps you need to work together to find the note for your next entry, unlike in simpler accompaniments where your note is played within the piano part.

A good example of this is in 'The Old Red Hills of Home' from *Parade* by Jason Robert Brown. Here, while the character of the young confederate soldier sings the smooth legato lines of a melody which has the essence of a simple American folk song, it is completely coloured by the ominous beat of distant drums summoning him to war. It is the piano that recreates those drums, their jagged staccato rhythms contradicting the calm of the sung melodic line. In this case the piano part is not so much an accompaniment which enhances the melody but rather an underscoring of the theatrical situation.

Accompaniments are usually a reduction and arrangement of what would be played by the orchestra, but really good accompanists seem to recreate the orchestral sound and instrumental colours from a

Jeff Edgerton – 'The Old Red Hills of Home' from *Parade* by Jason Robert Brown – Original Broadway Cast recording
and
Stuart Matthew Price with Bob Broad (piano) – in concert in Portsmouth, April 2010
The original Broadway recording transports us with its high-energy drum beat and marching band orchestration. This is the musical foundation that can inform you imaginatively and over which the vocal line must soar.

For the demonstration of how voice and piano must work together to tell a story and provide the same colours, watch the video recording of a concert performance by Stuart Matthew Price – who sang the role in the 2007 Donmar Warehouse production in London – here with pianist Bob Broad.

single keyboard. In songs where the accompaniment seems to work against the vocal line, it is even more important for the singer to be sure of the rhythm and the melody for in these instances your challenge is to stand alone and you should see this as a chance to really display your musical identity.

The capacity of music to create a number of simultaneous dialogues – which in complex ensembles can involve many different singers expressing their different personal thoughts at the same time – is one of its most exciting possibilities. The second act finale of Mozart's opera *The Marriage of Figaro* is perhaps the best of all examples of this. Over the course of twenty minutes, it develops from a duet, through trio, quartet, quintet and finally a septet as each new character enters the stage, adding a new element to the storyline and increasing the complexity of the situation. Each character sings their own thoughts, all at the same time but with perfect clarity. In working on music like this with a coach, the focus will be on ensuring the security of your own vocal line and character, while integrating seamlessly with the ensemble to further the overall dramatic picture.

The Marriage of Figaro Act 2 Finale by Mozart and Da Ponte – Metropolitan Opera Video, 1999

10
THE ACTOR'S SOLAR SYSTEM

The actor should always be at the centre of the song.

Making an analogy with the solar system, you are the sun, and the planets orbiting around you are all the influences on your performance of a song. The paths of the orbiting influences are directly related to your presence, and, to further the analogy, it is the burning flame of the sun (your passion) that gives light to the other planets. To achieve true technical freedom in singing, this life force is crucial and should never be distorted in order to seek truthful characterisation. The colour of the voice for characterisation should be regarded as a function of imagination – that is to say, an orbiting planet.

Other planets are composer, genre, lyricist, musical direction, style, the actors around you with whom you need to respond in the moment – in fact, all the legitimate influences on a song. These planets are lit up and put into orbit in the process of developing a performance in the studio and when the actor starts to sing in rehearsal or on stage, the song is a complex form of *play* with the joy of producing free and authentic vocal expression at the centre.

It is perfectly reasonable for the actor to keep a keen eye on the freedom of this function and indeed, once discovered, it is the actor's job to concentrate on maintaining this freedom while placing more and more planets into orbit. To reiterate, the voice should not be consciously coloured away from its central balanced quality – which the old Italians called chiaroscuro or light/dark. Vocal tone will receive colour and nuance as a function of the imaginative life of the actor.

Singing is not an attempt to *make* vocal tone, but to acknowledge it and communicate with it. The all-important truth in singing lies with the freedom of this instrument that makes tone. The greater the control over the production of voice, the freer the actor is to express themselves musically and theatrically. A fully fledged voice is a product of musicality, theatricality and a supreme physical and psychological self-control.

If vocal technique is seen as looking after this freedom, it need never be *hidden* or *forgotten*, as some methods suggest. The problem with 'forgetting' your technique is that in moments of self-doubt you either start to fall back on certain elements of technique in a negative way or actively try to forget it! Either way, in moments where we should be brilliantly free as an actor on stage, we can become tense and mannered.

Placing any of the orbital influences at the centre of the work is synonymous with masking the performance at its core. Ironically the actor is now less able to freely and imaginatively adopt the masks required to fulfil the needs of the theatre and the performance becomes bland and somewhat lifeless and characteristically lacks joy and spontaneity. When the actor has done sufficient work on freeing and controlling their instrument, an artistic validity can be established in their authentic tone.

Placing the genre of musical or theatrical expression at the centre is the most common mistake a beginner can make, and they can spend much of their effort manipulating the larynx to produce the tone that they believe is most highly regarded in terms of style, fashion or perhaps looked on favourably by prospective employers.

In the finest singing that we see and hear on stage, the end result is a complex reaction between many influences and not just a physical trick. Attempting to recreate a performance by means of trickery can often be really persuasive, particularly in young actors with naturally strong voices, but this pathway often leads to vocal trouble later. What is training if it does not aspire to be the foundation of a long and worthwhile career?

'Making tone is a killer' – Edward Brooks

'Singing without imagination is useless' – W. A. Aikin

11
ACTING THROUGH SONG

The marriage of music and lyric creates a dialogue expressed in an entirely unique way. As an actor, it's imperative to be able to explore the complexities of this wonderful dialogue in order to present a truthful, detailed representation of the character's inner workings and challenges as the composer intended. Without that detail, you're merely emoting.

Michael Peavoy – RADA Graduate

Jon Vickers – *Peter Grimes* (mad scene) Act 3 Scene 2 by Benjamin Britten and Montagu Slater – 1981 Covent Garden
'People that have been given a capacity, whatever it is, the capacity itself gets in the way…the capacity is not an end in itself.'

'(If)…you hold something so close to your eyeball, you blot out the universe.'

Both of these quotes come from one of the finest singer/actors of all time, the Canadian tenor, Jon Vickers. He has spoken eloquently in radio conversations about his realisation of the role of Peter Grimes and about the challenges of acting and singing. In the second quote he also expresses the importance for composers to 'let their work go' and allow others to interpret it.

The listening suggestion from *Peter Grimes* is written by the English composer Benjamin Britten in accompanied recitative form, where the text and the melody are intrinsically of equal importance. Vickers' singing and acting in this scene is an extraordinary illustration of everything we stand for in our work and in our book.

When technical understanding begins to develop and there is greater balance and ease in the voice, then you can relax into the work and learn to trust your actor's instinct.

'Half of interpretation lies in having the courage to leave things alone' – Harry Plunket Greene

Harry Plunket Greene – 'The Hurdy Gurdy Man' from *The Winter's Journey* by Franz Schubert and Wilhelm Müller, trans. Paul England – 1934

Harry Plunket Greene had a long and distinguished solo career, working closely with many leading British composers such as Edward Elgar, Arthur Somervell and Ralph Vaughan Williams, often premiering their work. Only a few recordings exist, but this interpretation of Schubert's 'Der Leiermann' – 'The Hurdy Gurdy Man', from *Die Winterreise*, recorded when Plunket Greene was 69, illustrates perfectly his desire to marry words and music.

When you sing songs, much of the 'acting' has been done before you get there by the lyricist and composer. They have directed you as to the rhythm, pitch, speed and dynamics. As the singer/interpreter, sometimes all you have to do is to connect and trust.

At this point you realize that actually *you* are at the centre of all this – not Shakespeare, not Mozart, not Sondheim! You are at the helm of the ship and now you are free to let your own imagination deepen the understanding of your audience. You must respect both the music and the poetry but you can and must be yourself, bringing your individual interpretation to the song you are performing.

Jessie Buckley in *Six Pictures of Lee Miller* by Jason Carr and Edward Kemp: RADA Production 2013. Photographer: Linda Carter

Here are some ideas that can help the research and development process of your song singing. Many of these will be familiar to you as ways in which, as an actor, you might prepare a script.

First familiarize yourself with background information:

- Research the historical, social and political context of the author/composer and the period in which the piece is set.

- If the song is from a musical, read the libretto or 'book' as you would if you were preparing a play script.

- Research other works by the same author/composer.

Working with the Words of a Song

- Study the text analytically. Ask the questions: Who are you? Where are you? What does your character need?

- Read the whole text, making sure you note the punctuation. It is a good idea to print off or write out the words for this purpose, separating them from the music.

- What makes your character sing the piece?

- What level of energy or agitation does the song begin and end with?

- Do a contemporary paraphrase of the whole song out loud.

- Speak the words as a monologue with your focus on storytelling, in your own accent.

- Speak the words as a monologue in the appropriate accent (go to a dialect coach to get expert advice on this).

- Underplay the scene.

- Overplay the scene.

- What would we not know about your character if the song was just a monologue without music, or even if it was cut from the show?

Some of the above may be legitimately done with script in hand. If you are struggling to remember the words you will be unable to engage fully with the exercise. Memorising words or music too early can hinder the ability to include your own nuance and deeper understanding of each word.

Now memorize the words.

- Line run at speed several times and either use a friend or a recording device to check that you are 100 per cent accurate. (A lot of this would happen naturally as part of the process of rehearsal with a director in a production, but you have to do this on your own for auditions and when you are learning new songs on your own.)

Working with the Notes of a Song

- Learn the notes and rhythms from the score. This sounds obvious, but if we had a pound for every time we had pulled a student up on this in a workshop or masterclass, we would be very wealthy indeed!

- You must learn the melody with accuracy. Play this on a keyboard or ask a pianist to record the melody line for you. Never try to learn a melody by listening to a recording of someone else singing it. Would you learn a speech from *Hamlet* this way?

- Look at the dynamic markings and observe musical instructions. Some of these markings may be in Italian – you can easily find out what they mean by checking them on the internet, or better still buy a book which covers the basic rudiments of musical terms and theory for reference.

- Use the Putting it all Together exercise on page 47, to explore all of the technical elements of singing the song.

- Think about the reason for the length of the notes. Why are some long and some short? Long notes sometimes indicate heightened emotion, although melody and rhythm can also be more abstract than this. Long notes are often the places where subtext can be more easily discernible and this is an opportunity for you to think through the long note – varying or developing your thought process as you go. This can have the effect of really bringing your performance to life. A long note is not an opportunity to switch onto automatic pilot while you think about the words for the next phrase or the location of the next breath. Do not just 'hold' the note. Let your imagination be in the moment, to develop the note and the ideas behind it as you sing it. A long note has the potential to have a story all of its own!

- What are the vowels on the long notes? Are any of them diphthongs? How will you negotiate these depending on accent and style?

- Look at the areas of the voice that the composer uses for different types of expression. It is often the case that the lower notes are used for storytelling and setting the scene, the medium notes for expression and the higher notes for exclamation. This mirrors what often happens in real life.

Your sound will be influenced by your imagination in a variety of ways. Small details in thought and subtext influence the tone in speech and song in the same way that changes of facial expression and body language imply a change of mood. Thought and emotionality have a profound effect on the voice.

Developing your artistry as a singer does not happen in any given timescale. It can happen in an instant or it may take years.

The BA students at RADA undertake a three-year training, and initially in their singing presentations we suggest their focus be split roughly 70/30 in favour of technique over performance. As they develop through their individual sessions and ongoing, informal presentations, we expect to see the balance shift, until by their final year everything is completely integrated.

While it may not be necessary to know the nuts and bolts of the musical language in every detail, being aware of music and musical form as well as rhythmic and melodic devices can only help you develop your artistry. Your coach can help you with this.

Here are some exercises to work on your song singing:

Writing the song

This exercise can be done unaccompanied or with a pianist absolutely following your chosen pace and rhythm.

Sit at a table and write down your text as you sing. Go slowly enough so that you can sing the words simultaneously with actually writing them down. It does not matter if the writing is only partially legible. Allow yourself to fully connect with your thoughts.

You can repeat this exercise and make a more theatrical version by looking up appropriately as if you are writing a letter on stage and sharing the contents with the audience. Explore how this changes the exercise for you.

See if your interpretation changes when you sing the song again without the imposition of the exercise.

Miming the song

Mime your song to a silent backing track playing in your head. Allow yourself to create a complete performance of the work minus any sound. Be aware of any internal physical movements that may occur. This is an indication that you are connecting mind and body in an organic way.

Let this experience of what happens within the body inform your performance of the song.

Second circle

Lottie Latham and Gunnar Cauthery in *Little Women* by Jason Howland, Mindi Dickstein and Allen Knee: RADA Production 2008. Photographer: Mick Hurdus

This idea works well with songs in which you are confiding in someone or telling them a story.

Sit opposite a fellow actor and play the scene in a very genuine way, first in speech, then in song. Be aware of your state when speaking the words. Is this the same state that you were in when singing? Should this be the case? What do you value about the nuance that you discovered in the speaking version? Bring this nuance to your singing.

Breaking barriers

An exercise inspired by our visit to the Boris Schukin School in Moscow in 2011. It taps creative energy in a student which may be blocked by fear and judgement. In this case this exercise might be employed as *technique in disguise*, as without vital energy and the appropriate mental approach to singing, some conventional techniques can be ineffective.

First, do a stock-in-trade version of your song. This is how you would expect that it would be performed by a stereotypical performer in the genre. Allow yourself to transform into the character that you choose. Perform the song in an imaginary space such as a jazz club, in the West End, at the opera house, at the music society gathering. Focus on stereotypical behaviour. Use a prop – a barstool perhaps, look out of the window (rain dripping down the pane), lean your back against the proscenium arch, move to centre stage, sing to the upper circle, sing to the gods, get creative!

Extend this by transforming into an overtly theatrical performer in the genre. Do not deny any impulses, allow for over-the-top expression, do not censor your imagination or physicality.

Now, embrace the physicality of these transformations and convince the listener that you are absolutely inhabiting them with your own voice and that you completely mean what you say.

It is worth saying here that very often the instruction to become stereotypical actually produces quite unexpectedly fine performances. This is perhaps the advantage of working with actors, but we feel that this exercise can be of great benefit, particularly when done for the first time!

The next stage in transformation is where the singing may become truly artistic. It is interesting in this stage how many actors instinctively stop manipulating the larynx and reveal a more authentic speech element in their vocalisation, although their character's dialect or accent may still be present.

It is crucial, as an actor, to develop the ability to understand the character through what the author, lyricist, librettist and composer have written down on paper.

Jules Massenet, the French romantic composer, wrote to Jean de Reszke after seeing him perform: 'You are unique in the role of Rodrigue, and you have a sincerity which no other will equal. It seems that you are really Rodrigue and Jean de Reszke at the same time.'

At RADA, I was encouraged to interpret songs through the eyes of a character, combining their psychology with the music, enabling a detailed emotional journey to take place in each song.

Brett Brown – RADA Graduate

Angela Lansbury – 'Not While I'm Around' from *Sweeney Todd* by Stephen Sondheim – with the Mormon Tabernacle Choir, 2002
An eminent student of the Webber Douglas Academy of Dramatic Art, singing with great musical and theatrical expression and demonstrating the importance of vocal technique both for vocal longevity and artistic development.

Johnny Depp as Sweeney Todd with RADA graduate Alan Rickman as Judge Turpin in *Sweeney Todd: The Demon Barber of Fleet Street* © 2007 DW Studio LLC and Warner Bros. Entertainment Inc. Licensed By: Warner Bros. Entertainment Inc. All Rights Reserved

Michael Ball as Sweeney Todd with RADA graduate Imelda Staunton as Mrs Lovett in *Sweeney Todd: The Demon Barber of Fleet Street* by Stephen Sondheim and Hugh Wheeler at the Chichester Festival Theatre 2011. Photographer: Tristram Kenton

12
MUSICAL FORM AND STORYTELLING

Andrea Riseborough in *Into the Woods* by Stephen Sondheim and James Lapine: RADA Production 2004.
Photographer: Mick Hurdus

As an actor you will already be familiar with the concepts of form and structure. In singing, because your tune pattern and rhythm are preordained, a song generally imposes a requirement of more precision from the performer than spoken text.

This following idea is an exercise to illustrate how the understanding of musical form can help to open up the composer and lyricist's intentions.

Taking a standard A-A-B-A song is a great way to start the exploration of how musical form can inform your acting. There are many types of musical form and this is just one of them.

A-A-B-A refers to the musical structure that the composer has used to set the words. A is the first melodic theme (often an eight-bar phrase), which is then repeated. B is a new musical theme (often referred to as the bridge) and then there is a reiteration of A.

The bridge

In the vast majority of cases, the last few words of the bridge (B section) encapsulate the whole reason why the song begins in the first place, so you can learn from this what your character most needs. This thought can replace any other thoughts that you might habituate to, such as: 'I wonder what they'll think of my voice?', 'How am I going to hit that top note?', 'Will I remember the words?'

Here are one or two examples of what we mean:

From 'I don't know how to love him' – the final bridge line is: 'What's it all about?'
From 'Cry Me a River' the final bridge line is: 'Told me you were through with me.'
From 'From this Moment On': 'Got the sweet lips to kiss me goodnight.'
From 'Love for Sale': 'Every love but true love.'
From 'Send in the Clowns': 'No one is there.'

Explore a variety of songs composed in this form and think about why the lyric at the end of the bridge is all-important.

Judi Dench – 'Send In The Clowns' from *A Little Night Music* by Stephen Sondheim – BBC South Bank Show, 1995
The concept of 'send in the clowns' comes from the multi-ring circus of late nineteenth-century America. When the American circus was still performed in a single ring there were just one or a few clowns and they were usually the star act. With the larger multi-ring performances the shows began hiring more clowns, however the emphasis shifted away from the clown acts. With multiple rings there were more difficulties in getting rigging ready in time, and with a larger cast, accidents were more likely to happen. So, it became standard practice to send in the clowns to fill any unexpected break in the show. In this context then, the words of this Sondheim masterpiece have a quality of desolation. Judi Dench gives a powerful and iconic performance, her characterisation of Desiree reflecting on the tragedy of her love life. The sense of loneliness in the last verse is palpable.

The gardener

This is an exercise which might help you to explore the storytelling nature of songs in standard A-A-B-A form.

Imagine the song as a most wonderful garden that you have nurtured for many years. Take the audience through the garden, the first A section or exposition being the first view of the garden. It almost always pays not to explain every plant but to let the garden speak for itself.

The repeat of A is another aspect of the garden. It should seem to be different from the first section. There are no rules here, but let your imagination change the interpretation of the first exposition of the melody.

The B section or bridge can be likened to a special place in this imaginary garden with a bench. This is where you explain why the garden exists and why you are a gardener in the first place.

The last A is a walk back. It is best not to prepare how you are going to sing the last A, but let your feelings derived from this journey release you emotionally and imaginatively.

The song will develop with your concentration and absorption in the music and the story. Make the stakes appropriately high. Most beginners suffer from setting low stakes and if you do not care, the likelihood is that the audience will not care either!

Explore your melody – imagine that you are the owner of a great Stradivarius violin, explore how this great instrument might colour your interpretation. Let your understanding of melody deepen and grow.

13
LISTENING AND THE VOICE AS A MUSICAL INSTRUMENT

Gemma Arterton as Elizabeth in the film *Song for Marion* – Steel Mill Productions 2012. Photographer: Nick Wall

When we asked Jason Robert Brown, one of the leading Musical Theatre composers of our generation, to write something for our book, this is what he thought was the important thing to say.

Acting through song is an enormous challenge for an actor; it requires as much attention to rhythm and intention as a Shakespeare monologue, with the additional demand of making music. Music does not just happen as a fortuitous result of producing the correct pitches; music must be made, and theatrical music can only be made with a true understanding of the way the text and the music combine (and sometimes work against each other) to tell a story.

Jason Robert Brown – Composer and Lyricist

Making music starts with acknowledging our singing voice as a musical instrument, and listening is a very important aspect of being a musician. We do not say to our students, 'don't listen to your sound', and we do not instruct them to listen to their sound either. Instructions such as these are over-simplistic and can lead to confusion. 'Don't think of pink elephants' can in some cases have the opposite effect! However, the concept needs some discussion, because for certain students, listening to yourself when singing can cause issues such as self-criticism, or can increase tension through trying to control the effect that the sound of your voice is having on the listener.

The word 'listen' suggests that we are interacting in some way with the origin of the sound [OED definition of listen: to give one's attention to a sound] as when we are listening to the birds, listening to the sound of the sea, listening to that annoying road drill or listening to Bach. This may be different from hearing [OED definition of hear: to perceive a sound].

If a sound is reasonably constant in volume and does not demand our attention with variations in its quality, then the brain can work to fade that sound into the background. We are aware of it, but we can easily focus on other things. We may become unaware of it completely until it stops! The reverse can also be true. In other words, if you are totally focused on other things to the exclusion of your voice as a musical instrument, then your sound may ultimately not demand your audience's attention and as a result may be rather constant and bland in its delivery.

Our perception of our own sound is not the same as that of our audience. Not only are we feeling the sound as well as hearing it, but also we have the phenomenon of the bone conduction of the vibration from the larynx to the ears to further complicate matters. Have you ever listened to the sound of your own speaking voice on a recording to be surprised by what you hear? In a wider sense we could also say that we can never fully know how someone else perceives us, and focusing on this is normally not a good idea in singing on stage.

We have spoken about the importance of a good working attitude when singing and our view that technique is based on centring the work on free and authentic vocal expression. The instruction not to listen creates a problem, because actively not listening means that we lose our freedom of choice. Not hearing or perceiving sound at all may prevent accurate musical tuning and music-making may be hugely compromised in every way. To maintain the optimum working state, we feel that you must be free to listen. However, we work to fill the mind with all the positive elements which allow for the greatest expression, so that any negative judgemental effects of listening are crowded out.

We should not actively subdue any of our senses in acting and least of all when making music. We should always feel free to interact with our sound, but because we value above all our freedom and authenticity, we cannot consciously dislodge our tone from its natural state, as this would be compromising the very freedom we so value. We can give our attention to the origin of the sound, because the origin of the sound is the true essence of ourselves and is physically absolute in accordance with nature. Absolute freedom to engage our free sound with whatever the music requires of us as actor/singers is of paramount importance.

Being free to interact with our voice in this way enables us therefore to sing musically and think of our voice as a musical instrument. In so doing we are expressing musical values with tone and not *making* tone as any sort of end product in itself. Tonal colour in singing, then, is a legitimate function of musical expression, itself connected with the imagination. Some commercial formulaic singers have a tendency to turn a song into a sort of *performance art* when their listening element is focused on how they want to be perceived. This is a long way from where we encourage you to be as actors.

We believe that music has a universal expression and certain fundamental elements of it can move us all in the same way. Stylistically though, we often react in polar opposite ways to music, which is why building your vocal technique around a style is not appropriate for an actor.

In our work, we find that the more the student becomes aware of the sensation of free tone and begins to gain in real confidence, then musicality begins to emerge as if it were there all the time. Greater ownership of the sound and a less judgemental attitude allows it to be part of the overall expression of the song. We instruct our students on various choices in musical phrasing when it is associated with a particular style, but find that it is more fulfilling for all parties when musicality develops as part of the technical process of freeing the voice.

Stravinsky, the great Russian composer, said that 'music is the highest of art forms because it is only about itself'. Provocative words perhaps; and it may be noted that Stravinsky's *The Rite of Spring* caused a riot after its first performance and remains one of the most visceral pieces of orchestral music ever written.

As previously mentioned, being exposed to expressive music and music-making can inspire greater expression in a student and we rely on our wonderful coaches, musical directors and accompanists to help us in this respect.

Musicality (your response to music in the way you shape it through breathing, phrasing and so forth) should not be confused with musicianship.

Musicianship is a term used for understanding the nuts and bolts of musical language. This is quite a different thing to musicality, although it is interesting that gaining knowledge in the language of music often gives a student more confidence as a singer, and greater musicality is often the result. Think of how it feels when you begin to know a little more than *hello*, *goodbye*, *please* and *thank you* in a foreign language. Little by little, it gives you more confidence to rely on yourself and make your own decisions.

An important element of musicality is rhythm. Rhythm is the soul of music, according to Harry Plunket Greene, and it is indeed our experience that some of the finest musicians that work with us at RADA have a fantastic and highly developed sense of beat, pace and attack. We have found that in our teaching, when the fear of singing is diminishing in our students, then greater musical attack and pulse becomes evident and a positive train of events begins to occur.

Stubby Kaye – 'Sit Down, You're Rockin' The Boat' from *Guys and Dolls* by Frank Loesser – Film, 1955
Stubby Kaye's tenor voice seems effortless right to its top and the chorus is brilliantly rhythmic and together. His musical attack is confident and superbly balanced. This performance is a great piece of Musical Theatre in its literal sense.

In a masterclass at RADA, Jason Robert Brown worked with one of our actors, Gunnar Cauthery, on the Rodgers and Hart song 'My Funny Valentine'. Jason asked him to express the melody as if his voice was an imaginary instrument – Gunnar chose a cello – and then encouraged him in various ways to 'extract the juice' from the melodic element of his song. This exercise intrigued us, and we wondered what the outcome might be. Allowing Gunnar to acknowledge his innate musicality through his phrasing as a separate entity from his acting skills, and actively use it as a special element of his overall process, enabled him to find yet another level of human expression when he put the song back together.

This exercise was yet another illustration of the very special way in which we are able to embody and express ourselves as human beings through our vocal instrument, our voice.

Joshua James, Jordan Mifsúd and Jake Mann in *Saturday Night* by Stephen Sondheim and Julius and Philip Epstein: RADA Production 2012. Photographer: Dave Agnew

14
AN APPROACH TO VOCAL AND THEATRICAL STYLES

Gemma Arterton and Ilan Goodman in *The Beggar's Opera* by John Gay and Johann Christoph Pepusch: RADA Production 2006. Photographer: Mick Hurdus

Singing is, for me, a fundamental tool in my acting kit. It enables one to communicate in a grander and deeper way. The fact that you have to engage your body and breath enables you to unlock impulses and emotions in an extraordinary way that isn't cerebral. Aside from the emotional release that singing can bring to actors, it is also important that an actor can sing In the profession. There is an abundance of fantastic material out there that is made wonderful by someone who can sing and act simultaneously.

Gemma Arterton – RADA Graduate

At RADA, we do not primarily focus on promoting a particular musical style or styles. If a particular style or genre is called for in a song or a production, we suggest that you undertake research into that genre, whether it be Opera, Jazz or German Weimar Cabaret, in the same way that as an actor you would research the background for a particular role – Shakespeare, Brecht or Sarah Kane. To find that style is a function of artistic creativity. The style or genre should never be a great wall in front of you to be scaled at your personal cost and vocal self-sacrifice, and it should not be a copy or pastiche of other performers.

Transformation in style and character for the singer comes in the same way that an actor preparing a role develops a characterisation through choices and direction.

RADA Graduate, Jonathan Pryce – 'The American Dream' from _Miss Saigon_ by Claude-Michel Schonberg and Alain Boublil – performed as part of Hey Mr Producer, a Royal Charity Gala at the Lyceum Theatre in London, 1998
Jonathan Pryce seems to play effortlessly with a song that sits high in the tenor voice. His energy is brilliantly high but his voice remains centred and he never pushes for volume or effect. A charismatic and mature performance, totally in control yet fully alive and in the moment.

Exploring the manner with which the character 'speaks' is a very important tool for getting your creative juices flowing; you can explore how it affects your sung tone. It may be that your character has an accent, it may be a particular vocal characteristic, age, or social class. There are specific theatrical styles which a musical director or director will want to adopt in particular circumstances – contemporary American Musical Theatre, traditional/period Shakespeare, perhaps Old Time Music Hall or stylized Restoration Comedy, to name but a few – and there will also be times when a director deliberately clashes styles to make a dramatic point.

Be aware that in this process you should not come to any conclusions or fixed vocal or psychological ideas before the rehearsal process starts. The multi-layered characterisation that you can develop in the rehearsal room might well elude you if you get there too soon.

In your own study of songs, be brave. Explore styles that are new to you. If the strong trunk of your tree represents your natural means of expression, then find the courage to advance down the branches towards their end. The further away from the trunk that you get, the thinner the branch becomes and the braver you need to be. The pay-off is that when you arrive back at the trunk then you have greater awareness of the span of the branches and the height of the canopy.

Some composers and musical styles will demand more theatrical and vocal transformation than others. For some students this can be quite liberating, while others will struggle with a particular quality. Be very aware that strong musical styles such as Rock will demand a great deal of vocal transformation, and you will have to naturalize and *own* your sung tone in order that your voice does not exhibit style over substance. Romantic operatic tone and contemporary belt are both quite extreme in their athletic vocal demands and these are examples of vocal style initially outside the realm of most actor/singers.

While these qualities can and should be studied by the more advanced student, the actor/singer may use these in performance but rarely make these tonalities their stock-in-trade. Certain styles, indeed, demand more vocally athletic performances, but basic technique remains the same and the necessary changes in musculature can and should be induced by the imagination.

For the actor/singer, musical style can either be seen as problematic or as a vital tool for expression, depending on your concept of vocal technique.

Openness of approach is critical in order to respond to the requirements of the text and to directorial choices. As an actor/singer you need to be ready to fulfil the demands of diverse productions. As an illustration, students in recent RADA productions have been asked to perform a German art song for a play set in the time of Byron – Howard Brenton's *Bloody Poetry*, an unaccompanied lullaby to a wished-for baby in Lorca's *Yerma*, some student-devised, high-energy songs telling the story of Peter Pan, and most recently a highly ornamented and very difficult English Baroque-style aria, written by the composer and musical director Gary Yershon for Congreve's restoration comedy *Love for Love*. All this alongside the production of a new musical, *Six Pictures of Lee Miller*, written by our current RADA Director Edward Kemp with music by Jason Carr. These are musical challenges that would not be out of place for first study singing students in a music conservatoire. We see similar challenges throughout the profession, and each challenge draws out more possibilities from each actor.

15
SOME STYLISTIC INFLUENCES

The style a composer chooses to write in may be either a development from or reaction to previous musical styles. A composer's authorial voice is a highly complex reaction of past styles and something inside them that they wish to express, consciously or subconsciously. As an actor, you have to be flexible enough to embrace a composer's style while staying true to your own impulses.

Molly Logan in *Saturday Night* by Stephen Sondheim and Julius and Philip Epstein: RADA Production 2012. Photographer: Linda Carter

Music is constantly being divided into genres and sub-genres that work as overarching and relatively arbitrary divisions. In classical music the divisions correspond to artistic time periods: Renaissance, Baroque, Classical and Romantic. In the twentieth and twenty-first centuries, genres overlap and are more stylistically based: consider Jazz, Pop, Blues, Hip Hop, Rap. Whatever the genre or period, or the overarching division, we see this as an umbrella definition which imposes on us an understanding of the type of music we would expect to hear. Most 'musical theatre' will fall into one of these categories, either through clear identification – Baroque Opera, Musical Comedy – or will fuse elements of these categories together to create a new hybrid style such as Hip Hop Opera.

It is interesting to look at some of the influences on major Musical Theatre names. Much of the work of Andrew Lloyd Webber is highly romantic, and it is possible to hear resonances of late Romantic era classical composers such as Puccini and Rachmaninov.

Musical style in Sondheim's work is very interesting in that his very particular authorial voice rubs shoulders with a plethora of musical styles of the past. Even in *A Little Night Music* he is unmistakable in his own expression, but one of his favourite composers, Maurice Ravel, seems to be consciously ever-present as well. Sondheim seems to thrive in his composition when the rigour of composing in past musical styles meets his need to express himself wholly and fully.

Jason Robert Brown is fascinated with the Baroque and fuses this with an R&B aesthetic to create a very distinctive authorial voice. Romanticism does not sit easily with his work with its obviously extrovert, heart-on-sleeve approach, and musical accuracy, melodic expression, vocal flexibility and a centred authenticity to the tone pays huge dividends in his songs. These are the hallmarks of the Baroque aesthetic.

Cole Porter, while being an obvious romantic, writes melodies that demand an elegance and profundity appropriate for the performance of some of the finest works of Mozart. This is just skimming the surface, but is at least a small illustration to provoke thought.

It is doubly important for an actor/singer, when meeting a strong style such as Jazz, Opera or contemporary American Musical Theatre, that your technique serves you well and that your authenticity is not swamped by the composer and the genre, making your performance one-dimensional.

As an actor, you can use style to your advantage. Think of it as a formal structure that is a polar opposite of freedom of choice. This creates a conflict out of which you might find greater expression.

Patsy Ferran, Gwyneth Keyworth and Emily Johnstone in *High Society* by Cole Porter and Arthur Kopit: RADA Production 2013. Photographer: Linda Carter

16
THOUGHTS ON REPERTOIRE

Despite being an extremely nervous singer, I found my singing lessons at RADA incredibly useful. Working one-to-one with my singing teacher every week was an immensely significant part of my training, giving me a deep foundation for all my voice work which I have never forgotten. The rigour and precision required, plus the extraordinary richness of the material to which one was introduced, allowed one to develop not only as a singer, but as an actor of heightened sensitivity, vocal facility, self-discipline, musicality, responsiveness to text and power.

Zoe Waites – RADA Graduate

The importance of studying the correct repertoire cannot be underestimated. Some of your repertoire will be chosen in order to work on long-term goals, some for medium-term goals and some in response to immediate needs for auditions, concerts or assessments. There is obviously some crossover between these areas.

As a general rule, try to study and perform the best songs from a genre. You can learn much about the art of singing from your teachers and coaches but also from the composers and lyricists of good repertoire. Our suggestions that follow are all fine examples of writing in their field.

Due to the nature of the training at RADA and the eclectic nature of the songs that our acting students are required to sing in both plays and musicals, the repertoire that we use to train our students is both varied and wide-ranging. Typically you could walk past a studio and hear an Italian operatic aria, an English lute song, a French art song, a bit of *Sweeney Todd* or *Parade* or perhaps something by Ed Sheeran or Adele.

The choice of repertoire for the first two years of training is almost always focused on the development of the voice from both a physical and psychological aspect. So while it may be felt that it is appropriate for one student to explore Sondheim, another might be singing Purcell, Mozart or Don Maclean. The most important aspect of the choice is that it is centred on the student's needs and serves to move the student towards greater vocal freedom and understanding.

Choosing songs in the wrong key for your voice can negate a lot of the good technical work that you are doing and can even lead to vocal deterioration as you force for top notes or strain due to singing in the wrong vocal tessitura (your comfortable average pitch area). Transpositions of songs for actors are sometimes acceptable as long as the key that is chosen is not too obscure and the reason for the transposition is not because there is something inherently wrong with your technique! Be aware that some vocal selection volumes may contain arrangements or transpositions of songs that are not in the original key.

You might choose to study a song that explores an area of voice that you are unaccustomed to; this might be in terms of range, or musical style. Alternatively, you might be building a repertoire for audition, the aim being to showcase your particular talents.

Have a balance of repertoire on the go so that your songs are not all very musically or technically demanding or all very high, low or overtly dramatic.

Lyrical repertoire which is based on legato lines is the staple diet for developing and demonstrating good vocal technique. A repertoire that does not contain a good number of melody-based songs might suggest a singer that is insecure or unstable vocally. Your personal choice of dramatic and character-based repertoire should be an extension from your lyrical repertoire. While these may be the songs chosen for audition repertoire, they should not make up the entire repertoire for study.

Singing can be very enjoyable, but enjoying a song is not always an indication that it is totally fit for purpose or is the one that best serves your needs! A great song can lead to vocal and artistic break-throughs. Make the most out of every song you study.

The list of songs which follows is by no means exhaustive, but might be a starting point for building a repertoire. We have included it here as a resource, rather than as a linear part of our book. You should dip in and out of it over time. Benefitting from one song might lead you to research others by the same composer or from the same genre or era. As your vocal technique improves, there is much pleasure to be found in singing more of the great works of art that were not at first accessible to your voice. Likewise your understanding of the lyrics may mature as you become more experienced and this can positively inform your singing as a whole.

Our grading of the songs from beginner through intermediate to advanced is only meant as a guide. To write 'beginner' next to a work of art makes us feel a little strange, to say the least! The singing voice is not like any other musical instrument. A beginner might be able to get through the phrases and sing all the notes of an advanced piece correctly, but unless their voice is settled, the story might be so distorted that it no longer fulfils the intention of the composer or lyricist. Conversely, in the hands of a great singer, a song labelled 'beginner' might become a highly complex and advanced piece of storytelling.

It is essential for the study of any foreign language song that you learn a word-for-word translation of the text. The English singing translations in most songbooks are not literal and will not sufficiently inform your work. It is also very important to be accurate with the pronunciation. With the Italian songs, take every opportunity to explore the value of the pure Italian vowels we mentioned earlier.

It is wise during your training and throughout your career to tackle many different styles and genres. You will learn something from everything you sing; it does not need to become your favourite song or even be that enjoyable! The benefit of studying a wide range of songs is that when you encounter different approaches and different material in the profession, you will have more points of reference to keep you centred.

Amarilli mia Bella
Giulio Caccini
Male or Female
Beginner
One of the earliest and most famous songs of the Arie Antiche – early Italian song – repertoire, 'Amarilli mia Bella' was part of a much bigger composition which Caccini called *Le Nuove Musiche* or *The New Music*. The melody lines in these songs were sung very simply with an effortless legato line and they were then to be ornamented by the performer, releasing the depth of expression inherent in the text. The

final phrase of the song offers the singer the most extraordinary opportunity to connect their technical ability to the expressive depths inherent within it. You might like to think of this song as a seventeenth-century precursor to 'Maria' from *West Side Story*.

Caccini gave a plethora of examples of vocal ornamentation in *Le Nuove Musiche*, but the modern-day singer more commonly sings the ornaments realized in editions such as the Schirmer *24 Italian Songs and Arias* and it is this book, which is available in either medium high or medium low keys, that we recommend. It is also available with a CD of piano accompaniments of all the songs printed in the book, which can be useful for practice.

Caro Mio Ben
Giuseppe Giordani
Male or Female
Beginner

Another famous Aria Antiche, and a very effective song for study, this is a very beautiful song which offers a challenge to singers from beginner to advanced because its apparent simplicity belies its emotional depths. Singing this repertoire is somewhat like exercising at the ballet barre and singers interested in all genres can learn much from the study of early Italian songwriters such as Giordani.

Fine Knacks for Ladies
John Dowland
Male or Female
Beginner

Especially good for male actor/singers and the young developing voice. The challenge in this song is its highly rhythmical nature. It can be effectively sung with a cockney accent as a character piece for an audition requiring this dialect.

I Attempt From Love's Sickness to Fly
Henry Purcell, text from John Dryden
Male or Female
Beginner

This song, by one of the finest English theatrical composers in history, is good for developing flexibility. The song should have a dance-like rhythm, and at the correct speed, the coloratura in this piece is neither too long nor too fast for the relative beginner. You need to approach these musical runs as a theatrical as well as a musical effect. The word-painting style, where the music reflects the literal meaning of the text, really benefits from an approach that is not overtly metronomic.

Come Again, Sweet Love
John Dowland
Male
Beginner

One of many Dowland songs well worth investigating. Word-painting is so evident in his works and this song is no exception. The rising sequential phrase, 'to see, to hear, to touch, to kiss, to die', has the voice raising the pitch with each thought and becoming more intimate and passionate. The long sustained note on 'die' is truly climactic! Word-painting can open the doors to singing for many actor/

singers, because melody composed in this style is not so much abstract but rather connected to the natural fall and rise of speech under various stimuli, both internal and external. This connection to the spoken word and to emotion can be a really useful learning tool.

Is It Really Me?
Harvey Schmidt and Tom Jones
Female
Beginner

A tender, romantic ballad which works well for the light soprano voice. As with most songs of a romantic nature, it is best to avoid sentimentality. Allow the voice to ring true. This song can be valuable for singing in the middle of the soprano range and is certainly potential audition material. It has no high notes but has a medium high tessitura.

I Can't Think What He Sees In Her
Vivian Ellis and A. P. Herbert
Female
Beginner

This is a very funny character piece which has the advantage of being little known. It is highly recommended for actor/singers and is a valuable English comedy song in any female singer's repertoire.

Say That We're Sweethearts Again
Earl K. Brent and Dorothy Shay
Male or Female
Beginner

This is a wonderful character piece, with a very funny lyric and a great character to inhabit. Verse two is spoken and needs to be well timed with the piano's rhapsodic treatment of the tune before the brief return of the theme and the climactic E flat at the end (which can be omitted for the octave lower if out of your range). This song is not well known and it might be hard to obtain a copy, but it is well worth finding.

Once Upon A Time
Charles Strouse and Lee Adams
Male
Beginner

A well-crafted baritone song suited to a more mature performer. It is not well known and is a good length for auditions. The ascending melody offers a good opportunity to work on release in the middle register.

I Won't Send Roses
Jerry Herman
Male
Beginner

This is a classic from the bass baritone Broadway repertoire and well worth studying in order to work on the middle register. This song can also be sung to good effect by higher voices when transposed into a suitable key. The song has a wistful, vulnerable quality.

And Her Mother Came Too
Ivor Novello and Dion Titheradge
Male
Beginner

This is a stylish and highly comedic piece which suits a light flexible vocal quality and an ease of delivery. This is a very good audition song from the English Musical Comedy repertoire.

She's A Woman
John Kander and Fred Ebb
Male
Beginner

Highly recommended for actor/singers. The melody is based on a repetitive pattern which offers a good basis for technical study. The strong character transformation is very useful for freeing some singers and the intensity of the message can help with the level of absorption in the song. As the song reaches its climax, there is a natural change from linguistic word stress to a vocal/musical stress pattern – in other words, higher notes are louder irrespective of word or syllable.

Johanna
Stephen Sondheim
Male
Beginner

A complex song that seems to give Anthony hero status, with the opening phrase being akin to the E flat leitmotif representing birth, which is heard at the beginning of Wagner's *Ring Cycle*. Sondheim is always challenging his audience, and here, the rescue of a damsel in distress, with its implied dominant and submissive characters, may be the issue that Sondheim is bringing to our attention through the somewhat dark and discordant music and lyrics.

  The song really benefits from a feeling of space and is a superb challenge for actor/singers as well as musical theatre performers. The vocal range is not extensive and does not exceed the E flat in the opening phrase, although this must be sung with an intense piano dynamic.

I Wish It So
Marc Blitzstein
Female
Beginner

A little-known song with a very memorable melody. It needs to be delivered with effortless beauty and when sung well it can reveal a big heart. This number can be sung by both sopranos and mezzo sopranos as the range is relatively small. It is a good audition song as well as being a useful tool for developing the often vulnerable middle range of the young female voice.

My Romance
Richard Rodgers and Lorenz Hart
Female
Beginner

As the title suggests, this is a highly romantic love song which is a good vehicle for the soprano or mezzo soprano voice. It has all the hallmarks of Rodgers and Hart – an effortlessly beautiful melody and a heartfelt lyric which is simple and elegant. It is a simplicity of approach that is the key to unlocking this classic standard.

Every Tear a Mother Cries
George Stiles and Anthony Drewe
Female
Beginner

A beautiful and moving contralto ballad by one of the most important contemporary English musical theatre writing teams. It has a universally understandable lyric and a romantic melodic structure. The tessitura is low and the song is best suited to more mature female voices. It is certainly suitable for audition.

Good Thing Going
Stephen Sondheim
Male
Beginner/Intermediate

An accessible song for a high baritone or tenor actor/singer, written in the style of the young student composer who sings it, with the feel of a light romantic pop ballad and touched with the genius of Sondheim. This is a good song for working on technique for the beginner or intermediate student.

Flow My Tears
John Dowland
Male or Female
Beginner/Intermediate

Another Dowland classic and perhaps his signature song. The falling phrases give the song a deeply melancholic quality. The language must be unpicked to make the thoughts clear to the performer and it may help to do a modern translation before going back to the early English. This is a song that can be sung effectively by all voices. The sustained nature of the melody makes it imperative that the voice is flexible and well produced and so this is a good song for learning these skills.

Unusual Way
Maury Yeston
Female
Beginner/Intermediate

An interesting composition with similarities to the Bach/Gounod 'Ave Maria'. Maury Yeston composes a beautiful romantic melody over a flowing Baroque-style accompaniment. It is a great piece to work on to show off a seamless legato line in the middle range of the voice. Care must be taken not to push the D sharp at the end which can result in singing sharp. This is a good song for the relative beginner and more advanced student alike.

My Funny Valentine
Richard Rodgers and Lorenz Hart
Male or Female
Beginner/Intermediate

One of the finest examples of its genre and a classic that should be studied by all aspiring actor/singers, this song has a beautifully constructed melody and a heartfelt lyric. This is not a particularly technical song but requires ease of tone and good legato to sing it well, not to mention a truthful delivery of that lyric!

Send In the Clowns
Stephen Sondheim
Female
Beginner/Advanced

Sondheim once joked in a London masterclass that he was going to do a medley of all his hits and proceeded to perform this, one of his most heartfelt songs. This remains his only song to make the popular song charts! Incredible, but an indication of the direction that he chose in order to express his artistry. His compositions are most certainly Art Music even if they do not obviously categorize themselves as such alongside other contemporary American theatrical music or Opera. Sondheim draws on such a wealth of knowledge of other styles and genres from the folk idiom to cabaret, from Irving Berlin pastiche to the contemporary American voice, from French impressionists such as Ravel and Debussy to our greatest theatre composers such as Purcell, Wagner and Tchaikovsky, and while his output effortlessly encompasses all, his songs always remain instantly recognisable as Sondheim.

It is worth singing this song in the original key of D flat with the monophonic lamenting introduction. It is certainly a low key to sing in, but it makes the song so much more profound. For people synaesthetically inclined, D flat feels so much more resonant of the story of this song than E flat.

Unfortunately 'Send In the Clowns' carries the burden of being the one number that people who cannot sing always do! It is therefore not advised as an audition piece unless you have extremely advanced acting skills, in which case the cynics may be totally turned around. Do not attempt to sing this song until you have worked on and have a clear and intimate understanding of the text and what is at stake for the character.

The Boy From
Mary Rodgers and Stephen Sondheim
Female
Intermediate

A fun character piece or patter song, offering the challenge of long phrases, perfect diction and delivery of a comic lyric.

Maybe I Like It This Way
Andrew Lippa
Female
Intermediate

Currently very popular so perhaps not one for auditions. A dramatic song that requires a good command of the middle register, although many young students cannot resist yelling the climactic section. Requires depth and truth to really do it justice.

Night and Day
Cole Porter
Male or Female
Intermediate

One of Cole Porter's finest songs and highly recommended for all singers. It begins with thirty-five repeated notes which perhaps indicates the intense nature of the lyric. Although it is the same note repeated, it is fascinating how the same note has to be recoloured each time in order to become part of the ever-changing harmonies that support it. Harmonically and melodically this song is exquisite and sensual and not technically too demanding.

How Could I Ever Know?
Lucy Simon and Marsha Norman
Female
Intermediate

One of the technical difficulties in this piece comes right at the beginning, where the singer's imagination must create the energy to express the text within a simple vocal line supported only by sparse accompaniment. Some singers will find the high F towards the end challenging, as this note usually lies above the bridge in the voice. The whole song does not sit too high so it is good for a developing soprano voice. It employs octave leaps and requires a good legato line.

I Don't Know How To Love Him
Tim Rice and Andrew Lloyd Webber
Female
Intermediate

A fabulous melody with an expressive Tim Rice lyric, this is certainly one of Lloyd Webber's finest songs. Its popularity offers a further challenge as an audition piece, but whether or not you use it in your audition repertoire, it is a great song to learn. The length of phrases and the ascending sixth in the melody will challenge certain students, so it can be a good technical study as well.

Wait A Bit
George Stiles and Anthony Drewe
Female
Intermediate

A beautiful song exhibiting both vulnerability and strength. It climaxes on a D, and this needs to be sung with a good forte. The ascending major seventh towards the end has its technical challenges also and is a lovely piece of word-painting. This is an opportunity to explore your dynamic range. Perhaps a classic English Song of the future?

Come To Your Senses
Jonathan Larson
Female
Intermediate

This is a driving contemporary song where the vocal line works well with the piano part and which has sensitivity as well as sheer drama. Not so high as some contemporary rock material, this song can be sung by actor/singers as well as high belt specialists. Has a great rhythmical catch in the delivery of the chorus.

Tell Me On A Sunday
Don Black and Andrew Lloyd Webber
Female
Intermediate

This song works really well for actor/singers, as the delivery of the lyric seems equally as important as the classic Lloyd Webber melody line. The large ascending intervals are a good study of the choices in phrasing; natural word stress succumbing to musical stress when the emotion is heightened. It is worth finding the score with the full ending as this is not printed in all editions. This song has a lower tessitura so is good for actors who are exploring their range and is ideally placed for mezzo sopranos.

Waiting For The Music
John Dempsey and Dana P. Rowe
Male or Female
Intermediate

Has a huge range, although the top C at the end is more of a special effect. If you have good top notes as well as a strong mid-range this can be a good showcase for your talents and because of that top C, it is not often performed. The theme of sexual awakening can be challenging dramatically.

Look What Happened to Mabel
Jerry Herman
Female
Intermediate

A vehicle for a star performance! This song needs careful rehearsal or a particularly sympathetic pianist if you are to achieve the ensemble in the 'colla voce' (with the voice) first verse. The technique of rhythmical breathing must be really good to keep the up-tempo verse sounding free and effortless, but when mastered the effect is well worthwhile. Not a big range but needs a strong forte on the last D.

Can That Boy Foxtrot
Stephen Sondheim
Female
Intermediate

Cut from *Follies*, this is a superb character piece in a pastiche cabaret style. Ideal for a more mature performer, it can also be performed by an accomplished younger actor/singer. The descending melody is a useful technical vehicle for working on vocal bridges in certain voices when sung in the higher printed key. Sassy, sophisticated and humorous.

George
William Bolcom and Arnold Weinstein
Male or Female
Intermediate

A wonderful and virtually unknown character piece by an American composer whose works are well worth exploring to discover further repertoire. This is one of his many fabulous cabaret songs and is a great tool for an accomplished actor/singer who has a good feel for musical style and a flair for the darkly comic.

Giants In The Sky
Stephen Sondheim
Male
Intermediate

A highly rhythmical and energized patter song with a Sondheim lyric and a soaring melody, this song offers an opportunity for technical study as well as being a good audition piece. It should be in the repertoire of every light young tenor voice. Brilliant.

Don't Take Much
Cy Coleman and Ira Gasman
Male
Intermediate

A dark and sinister dramatic baritone song, which has a wide range to top F sharp, and which needs a good sinuous legato line. Shows the voice off well and is potentially good audition material.

King David
Herbert Howells and Walter de la Mare
Male or Female
Intermediate

An extraordinary song in the English art song repertoire. Highly pictorial, both text and music are of a narrative nature. The song has a quality resembling sustained accompanied recitative and is based firmly in the word-painting style. Howells would ask his composition students at the Royal College of Music to speak the words of the poem and observe both the natural rise and fall of the spoken pitch and the relative length of the words. This exercise was to inform the melody line – the spoken tone being dependent on imagination and theatricality. Harmonically this song has a wonderful tonal palette, from the first chord to the key change to E major.

Where the hundred harps in the poem begin to play, the music evokes a vision of the doors to a great hall opening to reveal this fantastical occasion, almost as if you were opening a children's picture book. Allow yourself to make your images in this song very colourful, and to explore how the song is changed through using a childlike imagination. As always, the message of the song needs to be teased out of the text for the performance to be complete.

Lascia Ch'io Pianga
George Frederick Handel and Giacomo Rossi
Female
Intermediate

A beautiful and majestic Handel aria that is accessible to actor/singers as well as classically trained voices. It is available in various keys and so can be sung by all female voices. As with many Handel arias it needs a good legato line and even tone throughout the range. This is in essence why Handel is a great composer to study, as his work can be very beneficial for the development of this most crucial aspect of singing.

Where'er You Walk
George Frederick Handel and William Congreve
Male
Intermediate

A highly recommended piece for the development of the young tenor voice. The major seventh leaps to F sharp in the middle section offer a real challenge to technical command of the passaggio. This aria is melodically quite simple so it is suitable for singers from the relative beginner to the most advanced. Vocal range to high G.

Who is Sylvia?
Franz Schubert, text from William Shakespeare
Male or Female
Intermediate

A Schubert song that offers a really worthwhile opportunity for technical study. In B flat (the tenor key) the leaps towards the end of the melodic line are good for working on the passaggio.

Roses
Stephen Adams and Fred Weatherly
Male
Intermediate

An Edwardian song that is claimed to have been instrumental in launching the career of the Irish lyric tenor John McCormack. It is beautifully written for the tenor voice and is very rewarding to sing. There is an option of singing a strong top A on the anti-penultimate note of the song. As the title suggests, the song is romantic in its nature, but does not feel musically too sweet or sentimental. This could be a very useful audition piece as it is relatively unknown and shows the voice off well.

Roses of Picardy
Haydn Wood and Fred Weatherly
Male
Intermediate

One of the most popular songs of the Second World War and with a lyric penned by the prolific Fred Weatherly, this is a romantic ballad with a superb flowing melody and expressive intervals. It is most suited to the tenor voice although it could be transposed to suit a lyric baritone. The robust nature of the melody and the style ensures that this song does not stray too much towards the sentimental. Highly recommended for tenors and potentially a good audition piece.

The Cloths of Heaven
Thomas Dunhill and W. B. Yeats
Male or Female
Intermediate

By a little-known composer, this delicate song has a very tender and vulnerable lyric. It has a beautifully expressive mezza voce ending which requires good technical control. It is short so is ideal for audition but perhaps only for the more experienced singer, as its delicate nature might be adversely affected by nervous tension.

L'Heure Exquise
Reynaldo Hahn and Paul Verlaine
Male or Female
Intermediate

A beautiful and sensual French melodie, this song is wonderfully expressive and tender and needs an intensity and relaxation in the soft dynamic. As can be expected in romantic French repertoire, the piano part provides a harmonic structure that is integral to the mood of the song, so there needs to be good rapport between singer and accompanist. This is a good concert piece.

Lorelei
George and Ira Gershwin
Female
Intermediate

An amusing female character song suited to maturity and benefiting from confidence and easy sexuality. The melody has quite a wide range and requires a good flexible middle register. A useful piece for audition, this is classic Gershwin.

Someone To Watch Over Me
George and Ira Gershwin
Female
Intermediate

Originally a soprano song, this is a classic jazz standard that has been sung in many keys and published in many editions. It works beautifully for the light soprano and needs an ease in the higher middle register. In this higher tessitura the beauty and flexibility of the voice is all-important but in the versions for lower voices, the delivery of the lyric becomes more important as the voice is nearer in quality to spoken tone.

The Old Red Hills of Home
Jason Robert Brown
Male (Tenor)
Intermediate

A great contemporary romantic ballad which becomes more dramatic as the song progresses. The melody and implied harmonic structure is very much rooted in American folk song, although the piano provides an ominous and sometimes discordant drum beat. This creates both musical drive and dramatic conflict contrasting with the simplicity of the melody and honourable youthful lyric. A very good song for a young tenor both for developing the art of song singing and for audition, although the piano part is quite tricky to sight-read. A useful vehicle for exploring the relationship between emotionality and freedom of vocal production.

It's Hard to Speak My Heart
Jason Robert Brown
Male
Intermediate

This dramatic ballad needs good legato line and a light floated top. The composer marks the top E naturals to be sung falsetto, which highlights the emotional complexity. Great for audition, as this contemporary song is short and has a simple but atmospheric piano part.

All the Things You Are
Jerome Kern and Oscar Hammerstein
Male
Intermediate

A classic musical theatre tenor ballad, from a composer known for his melodic gift. The extension to the melody at the end of the song can demonstrate good range but the tessitura is relatively low and so the song is not as technically demanding as it might sound. An excellent audition piece for a tenor with an easy, well-supported top A flat.

Stormy Weather
Harold Arlen and Ted Koehler
Male or Female
Intermediate

A jazz standard that is very well written for the young male voice, as its range is not too extensive. It moves languidly in the middle register, aiding the development of a good legato. It is therefore recommended for study as well as being a good piece for audition. As with a lot of jazz-based songs, the feeling of style should not dominate the performance but should be an effortless, positive component.

If You Could See Her
John Kander and Fred Ebb
Male (Tenor)
Intermediate

A great character piece for the tenor voice. The elegance of the melody makes the piece ideal for study and the subject matter is both interesting and provocative. The range is quite extensive, compassing a high A flat on the top, although this can be taken in falsetto if necessary. A good audition piece.

I'm Not Afraid of Anything
Jason Robert Brown
Female
Intermediate

A good example of a Jason Robert Brown female ballad. As with many of his songs, this is a fusion of Baroque musical intricacy with rhythm and blues style and sensibility. The result is a unique voice, contemporary but musically and rhythmically as demanding as Bach! Jason Robert Brown's songs tend to be very long, so they are not normally recommended for audition unless specifically requested.

I Know Things Now
Stephen Sondheim
Female
Intermediate

A superb character song for a young actress, which is driven by highly rhythmical music and a dark intricate lyric. The main theme has a playground song quality, but the middle section is harmonically and melodically challenging and extends the range up to high E. Do not allow the musical challenge of the bridge to put you off. The tonally shifting melody in this section, which can at first seem really tricky, becomes second nature with enough practice. As with many Sondheim songs, this is challenging and rewarding on many levels.

Losing My Mind
Stephen Sondheim
Female or Male
Intermediate

One of the finest songs in the musical theatre genre, it is found in two keys and is suitable for soprano or baritone in the higher (E flat) with the original key of B major suiting most lower female voices. The musical structure creates an extraordinary depth of tragic expression while intriguingly remaining in the major key. The piano interludes give the singer time to contemplate the next thought and in the context of the song, time seems magnified and serves to increase the emotionality. A mature piece, this song has suffered from overexposure, so be careful if using it for auditions. It is well worth learning as it can help development on many levels.

If I Loved You
Richard Rodgers and Oscar Hammerstein
Male or Female
Intermediate

A very popular romantic ballad by one of the most extraordinary writer/composer teams in musical theatre history, Richard Rodgers' melodic gift is central to this classic song. Sung well, it is a great vehicle to display a well-balanced instrument over an extended range. The ascending phrase at the end, rising to the top G flat, is particularly challenging, as the climax needs a sustained 'u' vowel which in most voices becomes modified at this pitch range.

Everybody Loves Louis
Stephen Sondheim
Female
Intermediate/Advanced

As with all Sondheim's songs, you get out what you put in, and more! Sondheim has constructed a superb monologue which reveals the character's innermost thoughts of tenderness and frustration. Learning the rhythm accurately at the outset is essential, as it is always so much harder to correct errors at a later date. When prepared well, this song is one of those gifts that seems to bring out the best in a performer and so for the right situation it can be a good audition piece, although the piano part is tricky to sight-read. This song sits for the most part in the lower middle of the voice.

Love For Sale
Cole Porter
Female
Intermediate/Advanced

Another Cole Porter masterpiece, with an interesting and controversial history, due to the challenging lyrics. Although the original key may place it too high for some voices, there is a printed version in the songbook of the film 'De-Lovely' which allows lower voices to study this great song. In the normal printed key, the melody has a wide range and can be highly demanding, especially the quasi-cadenza or vocal ornamentation at the end. When viewed theatrically as well as musically, this cadenza is a good tool for improving support for the upper register.

The Ladies Who Lunch
Stephen Sondheim
Female
Intermediate/Advanced

A gritty Sondheim ballad. Stylish, cynical, mature and highly dramatic in nature, this is a great song for the actor/singer who sings well in a spoken range or for the singer wanting to develop the lower register of the voice. The song climaxes on repeated fortissimo notes which need real exclamatory quality.

Surabaya Johnny
Kurt Weill and Bertolt Brecht
Female
Advanced

A song of real substance. The melody is wide-ranging, and to sing it requires an accomplished technique as well as great dramatic potential. Although printed in E flat, you could try singing it in C if your voice does not comfortably bridge the top notes. Do not worry about the line 'there's an old woman staring back at me', unless you appear very young, as Weill's character in this song is not particularly old!

The Light in The Piazza
Adam Guettel
Female
Advanced

An excellent song for young soprano voices, romantic and soaring with a contemporary feel. In the higher of the two keys, D, it requires an open and expressive tone up to F sharp which can be challenging, but which is rewarding when mastered. The piano part is tricky so this is not a particularly good choice for auditions, especially in the higher key.

Astonishing
Jason Howland and Mindi Dickstein
Male and Female
Advanced

A superb end-of-act-one rousing ballad. If sung well, this song showcases the talent of a young leading singer. It requires musical sensitivity and immaculate phrasing as well as considerable range and power. If you have the necessary talent to take this on, try to avoid a copycat performance. There is a natural cut for audition purposes.

No Good Deed
Stephen Schwartz
Female
Advanced

A well-constructed song, which for the right singer can be a true tour de force, this is a dramatic ballad requiring a big voice and an advanced technical ability. You should avoid this type of song until you feel ready for the specific challenge, as this repertoire can be quite vocally destructive if the voice is driven.

What Good Would The Moon Be
Kurt Weill and Langston Hughes
Female
Advanced

Kurt Weill at his romantic Broadway best. A beautiful melody with a classical soprano range and heartfelt pathos. A good audition piece for a strong soprano.

Gethsemane
Tim Rice and Andrew Lloyd Webber
Male
Advanced

One of Lloyd Webber's best dramatic songs. This piece is often sung by students who are a little over-optimistic of their technical ability and in these cases it can be quite destructive. For an advanced tenor with a good top, this is a fabulous song to connect technical virtuosity with theatrical transformation and truth.

Lonely House
Kurt Weill and Langston Hughes
Male
Advanced

In the original key this is a great song for a tenor to explore the passaggio. It has a top B flat at the end which should be sung in a mixed voice quality and not in pure falsetto. This is a fabulous song with a heavy blues feel and a plaintive melody. In the lower key it is accessible for the baritone voice but lacks the haunting quality that the high tessitura offers. A good audition song for the advanced singer.

Why God Why?
Claude-Michel Schonberg and Alain Boublil
Male (Tenor)
Advanced

Ultra-romantic in nature and with a high tenor tessitura, as an audition piece this is best sung only by the most able. However, it is a good song for all singers who want to work on the top of the tenor range. As with all romantic songs, it will really suffer if the sentiment is played to the detriment of the truth of the character and situation.

Sarah
Frank Wildhorn and Jack Murphy
Male (Tenor)
Advanced

Another modern American romantic piece. The key change takes the voice up to a B flat and the second verse sits quite high in the range. This can be a very effective song, although ease of production and quality of tone need to be spot on to unlock the beauty in this contemporary ballad. A good audition piece for a young, advanced, high tenor.

Lenski's Aria from *Eugene Onegin*
Pyotr Ilyich Tchaikovsky
Male (Tenor)
Advanced

One of the finest operatic tenor arias ever written. Melodically haunting, the falling phrases are typical of Tchaikovsky's heartfelt expression and offer a superb vehicle for an advanced tenor voice. The range only goes up to high A flat, so this piece should not put a strain on the top of the voice. It is recommended to sing the aria in Russian as the vowel sounds can be useful when working on passaggio notes.

Waft her Angels
George Frederick Handel and Rev. Thomas Morell
Male (Tenor)
Advanced

A heartbreaking piece with an exquisite melody, it is particularly appropriate for a high tenor with an ability to float the top of the voice, offering long ascending phrases which mirror the ascent of the soul into heaven. It is an excellent vehicle for displaying technical virtuosity in breath control and ease in the upper register.

I Hear You Calling Me
Charles Marshall and Harold Lake
Male
Advanced

Charles Marshall is a relatively obscure composer and this is his greatest song. It was John McCormack's signature tune and his wife Lily used the title for her biography of her husband in 1950. It is a most expressive song which ideally suits a tenor with good technique and an ability to sing a beautiful mezza voce on the top. Although not written, the last phrase is crying out to rise up to a pianissimo A flat. It needs a performance with good stylistic taste and is a great opportunity to display vocal and technical excellence.

Oh Quand Je Dors
Franz Liszt, text after Victor Hugo
Male or Female
Advanced

Suitable for sopranos and tenors, this is an exquisite romantic masterpiece, which should only be sung by technically advanced students. It has an extraordinary feeling of timelessness and space.

L'Invitation Au Voyage
Henri Duparc and Charles Baudelaire
Male or Female
Advanced

This is a fantastic romantic song for the higher voice. The piano part creates real dynamic and theatrical tension and the impressionist harmonies are quite extraordinary in their expression.

Sweeter Than Roses
Henry Purcell
Male or Female
Advanced

A passionate, sensual outpouring which is highly recommended for study. One of the finest early English songs, it can be sung by all voice types and is of advanced difficulty, encompassing the lyrically exquisite to the dramatic coloratura. The sensual nature of the song can be good for the actor/singer to make connection between the technical and imaginative aspects of performance.

You Don't Know This Man
Jason Robert Brown
Female
Advanced

A contemporary dramatic ballad which needs a strong even tone up to E flat. This is sometimes a challenge if you are forcing the chest register upwards. To avoid this, the passaggio, which occurs around the B natural in some female voices, should be explored. This is one of Jason Robert Brown's shorter songs and is therefore more suitable for auditions than his longer compositions.

Evermore Without You
David Zippel and Andrew Lloyd Webber
Male (Tenor)
Advanced

An excellent piece for a robust tenor voice, this is Lloyd Webber at his romantic best. The song has an operatic quality similar to a Puccini aria and the range is similarly wide-ranging. A good exercise for an advanced singer, which will expose any flaws in vocal technique.

On The Steps Of The Palace
Stephen Sondheim
Female
Advanced

A very rhythmical song with an extraordinarily complex lyric and rhyme scheme which gives the character of Cinderella a stratospheric intellectual status! Sondheim's Cinderella is capable of incredible linguistic expression, so ensure that you fully understand her thoughts before performing this very effective and amusing piece. This is a really challenging song and needs learning correctly first time round as mistakes in the rhythm will be really difficult to rectify.

Being Alive
Stephen Sondheim
Male
Advanced

The climax of Sondheim's *Company*, this is a cathartic outpouring of an epic nature. This is a highly challenging piece both physically and emotionally and is an excellent piece for an aspiring tenor or high baritone to study. In its full show version this song has a demanding operatic tenor range and physical scope. Despite this, the song is cut and transposed up in *All Sondheim Volume One*! The song is also available in a lower key but it is a better piece for the greater physical and psychological challenge afforded by the original version. This is a very popular piece, so do be wary about which auditions you use it for.

Patterns
Richard Maltby and David Shire
Female
Advanced
Reminiscent of some Sondheim songs, this piece uses repetition to bind the character to their situation. The repeating melody, which sits in the middle register of the female range, demands real vocal and imaginative maturity to fully flesh out the song and give the piece the heartfelt quality it demands. A great piece for the right singer, but a real challenge.

The Girl In 14G
Jeanine Tesori and Dick Scanlan
Female
Advanced
A showstopper! The singer must demonstrate a chameleon-like quality, taking on the three separate personas in the piece: the character herself, the opera singer upstairs and the blues singer downstairs, all of whom have wildly different vocal colour and range. This can be a real vehicle for a star performance and a great encore piece for a concert.

Additional Suggestions

Further to this first list of specific repertoire, here are some thoughts on how you might extend your research to explore additional suggestions in foreign languages. These ideas are only meant as a starter and you might want to venture into other avenues, such as French Art Song or Chanson. Some extra repertoire is suggested under the following headings.

German Lieder and the song cycle

No repertoire list for studying the art of song singing should omit the great German songwriters whose works are among the finest masterpieces of all time and have inspired generations of songwriters. We have included some German art songs (Lieder) in the primary list. This repertoire is generally not the staple diet of our students and we do not introduce these songs until the student has a good grasp of basic technique.

As they progress, students may familiarize themselves with the major song cycles of Schubert and Schumann to broaden their knowledge base and to be inspired by the craft of these great masters. When studying this repertoire, the songs should be learned in German as well as English. This will inform the transformative quality that these songs require.

A song cycle is a succession of songs which tell an overarching story. The stories centre themselves on fundamental areas of human experience, such as love, companionship and death. Some of the greatest Lieder singers seem to reach a transcendental state in the performance of these works, finding themselves totally immersed in the character's journey. Four of the most well-known song cycles from the Romantic Period are Franz Schubert's *Die Schöne Müllerin* (The Beautiful Maid of the Mill) and *Winterreise* (Winter Journey) and Robert Schumann's *Dichterliebe* (A Poet's Love), all written for male singers, and *Frauenliebe und Leben* (A Woman's Life and Love) written for female voice, also by Robert Schumann.

Der Nussbaum
Robert Schumann and Julius Mosen
Male or Female
Beginner
A simple Schumann song, with a delightful romantic innocence, it demands an even sustained tone in the middle range when sung in the low key, making it a good vocal exercise for those female voices wanting to work on this part of the voice. The phrases are not too long and so make the song appropriate for the beginner as well as the intermediate singer. The piano part is typical of Schumann, as it does not just provide accompaniment for the vocal line, but plays a prominent part in the communication of the overall story.

Ständchen
Franz Schubert and Ludwig Rellstab
Male or Female
Intermediate
Ständchen or Serenade has a sublime melody and is suitable for all voices, although the range is quite extensive. It is important to have a good top to the voice in order to sing it most effectively. The song is highly romantic in character and illustrates how Schubert crosses the boundary between Classical and Romantic expression. Listen to recordings of Fritz Wunderlich and Elly Ameling singing Lieder to appreciate an elegance of tone and phrasing in music of this period.

Ich Grolle Nicht
Robert Schumann and Heinrich Heine
Male
Intermediate
From Schumann's *Dichterliebe*, this is a truly dramatic short song, ideal for high baritones, which demands great technical control and a feeling of inner rage. There is an optional top note at the end which is equally effective if taken, as Schumann suggested, by the piano alone, although singers blessed with great top notes have never been able to resist it!

Heidenröslein
Franz Schubert and Johann Wolfgang von Goethe
Male or Female
Intermediate
A short strophic song with a lyric by Goethe which speaks metaphorically of the plight of the slighted lover. The melody is in the major key and has an implicit grace and charm. It moves the voice well and the penultimate phrase is a challenging rising scale to a sustained high note. When sung in German this rising phrase peaks on the word 'rot', meaning red. The German pronunciation of this word might

help some singers to keep their larynx in a better position while singing high notes. This song is not particularly sustained and so is a good exercise for the intermediate singer seeking to develop flexibility and range.

Der Neugierige
Franz Schubert and Johann Wolfgang von Goethe
Male
Advanced
An exquisite short song for a male singer with a light classical touch, containing long lines of sublime melody and ideal for showing off a beautiful lyrical voice. Be aware that a song with these elements demands a strong and secure core in order to be successfully delivered and so this is recommended only for the more advanced singer.

Mondnacht
Robert Schumann and Joseph Eichendorf
Male or Female
Advanced
One of the most beautiful and most difficult songs ever written, and for the very advanced singer makes a wonderful addition to a concert programme. Schumann's expressively chromatic piano part is integral to the mysterious wonder of this miniature masterpiece.

Operatic arias

The perception of the operatic aria is that it is not the usual repertoire of the actor/singer. Most of the well-known Romantic era operatic roles are written with an extensive range and demand great vocal athleticism stemming from a secure and flexible core structure. Certainly these roles are only suitable for advanced singers with a good grasp of vocal technique and a strong voice. However it is important to remember that Opera is the combination of music and theatre and many individual arias, particularly from early opera, can provide a valuable basis for technical study for all singers.

The Arie Antiche, to which we referred earlier in this chapter, were in many cases written with vocal development in mind. The pitch range of most of these songs is movable but the intention was that they should explore the lower middle to upper middle areas of the voice, which are hugely important in the development of technical mastery. With many of these early arias the embellishment of the simple melodic line was left to the singer, who was expected to decorate it in an improvisational way to create their unique performance of the song in the moment. This has similarities to jazz, where the music has a strict form in terms of harmonic structure and overarching rhythm but where the performer feels free to respond in the moment, musically and dramatically.

As well as the Arie Antiche repertoire, there are a number of arias that can be studied to good effect by the actor/singer. Here are some ideas.

Papageno's Aria (Der Vogelfänger) from *The Magic Flute*
Wolfgang Amadeus Mozart and Emanuel Schikenader
Male (Baritone)
Beginner/ Intermediate

An operatic aria written specifically for an actor/singer – the first performer, and the opera's librettist, was the theatre actor Emanuel Schikenader. This is a great starting aria for a baritone looking to develop his repertoire in this area. It is playful and not highly sustained or highly emotive and so is suitable for all levels of ability.

Deh Vieni Alla Finestra from *Don Giovanni*
Wolfgang Amadeus Mozart and Lorenzo Da Ponte
Male (Baritone)
Beginner /Intermediate

A canzonetta of lyrical charm and theatrical simplicity as the Don sings a serenade in order to get his wicked way. It should have a seductive ease and a well-centred vocal placement.

Che Faro Senza Euridice from *Orfeo*
Christoph Willibald Gluck and Rainieri de' Calzabigi
Female (Mezzo Soprano) or Male (Counter Tenor)
Intermediate

The arpeggio based melody in this aria makes this very expressive piece a great exercise for working on vocal technique. Originally Gluck conceived it for a castrato or male soprano voice, and it is ideally suited to voices that exhibit warmth in their middle range. The Orpheus myth has always been a popular operatic theme, and the sentiment in the text is deeply heartfelt. The vocal climaxes at the end to the high F are very effective when sung with a strong, well-produced ringing tone.

O Mio Babbino Caro from *Gianni Schicchi*
Giacomo Puccini and Giovaccino Forzano
Female (Soprano)
Intermediate/Advanced

A very well-known aria and one of the few in this romantic genre that is accessible for the actor/singer with a strong soprano voice. The aria is sung by a young character and Puccini has kept both the vocal and dynamic range within manageable limits. The phrases are quite long and demand good command of the breath, especially for the A flat octave leaps. There is also some use of portamenti in this aria, a device commonly used in this period to carry the voice expressively from one note to the next. Recommended for intermediate and advanced students looking for a vocal challenge.

Deh Vieni, Non Tardar from *The Marriage of Figaro*
Wolfgang Amadeus Mozart and Lorenzo Da Ponte
Female (Soprano)
Advanced

A beautiful song of longing and desire, which in the context of the opera contains a double meaning, as Susanna seems to sing for a lover, knowing all the time that her fiancé, who is hiding nearby, will overhear and misunderstand. This offers wonderful opportunities for sung characterisation. The range goes to a high A but does not demand a dramatically coloured tone. The use of arpeggios to shape the musical line is simplicity itself and Mozart fits music to character perfectly. Despite its seeming simplicity, this aria demands excellent control of the vocal range and breath.

Ach, Ich Fühl's from *The Magic Flute*
Wolfgang Amadeus Mozart and Emanuel Schikenader
Female (Soprano)
Advanced

A perfect musical and vocal expression of heartbreak and desolation. Mozart places the melody in a very high vocal tessitura as Pamina expresses all the conflicting emotions of her complex situation through achingly long and heart-wrenching musical phrases. The greater the control a soprano has of the core structure of her voice, the greater the spectrum of colour and dynamic range she can use to express herself in this very demanding tessitura.

The Laughing Song from *Die Fledermaus*
Johann Strauss with Karl Haffner and Richard Genée
Female (High Soprano)
Advanced

This is a character piece that is virtuosic and a great opportunity to demonstrate agility and ease in the upper vocal range. It has elegance and a real sense of style as Adele the maid tries to convince us all that she is of noble descent! This aria needs some staccato singing, as the laughing in the title suggests, and contains a sustained high D in altissimo at the climax.

Habanera from *Carmen*
Georges Bizet with Henri Meihac and Ludovic Halévy
Female (Mezzo Soprano)
Advanced

A classic of the operatic repertoire, this is a great song for female actor/singers looking to explore operatic expression. The Spanish dance rhythm can give the singer a feeling of energy. When sung in French, the vowel sound on 'l'amour' can help with the necessary timbre for the high E at this point in the melody. You might like to make comparison with the same aria in *Carmen Jones*, where the English words 'Dat's Love' bring a different colour to the identical melodic line. A great piece if one can avoid the sexually clichéd veneer that can so often be the singer's downfall in this piece, leading to the trap of focusing on style over substance!

17
UNACCOMPANIED SINGING

Unaccompanied singing is not as easy as it may first seem. Granted, you have only yourself to think about, but you are solely responsible for so many things.

- Starting on the right note.

  The way to prepare for this is to either be given a note or to find another way of approximating your starting note. For example, if you know that the first note is the lowest you sing in the piece, it pays to start on a comfortable but lowish note, so as not to find that the higher notes in the song are too high.

- Keeping the rhythm and setting the pace.

  Rhythm is very important in music, but it can be varied as long as the overall structure is kept in place. Because you do not have to keep time with anyone else, you should find a natural rhythm and pace for the song that suits you and the delivery of the song. You are in control of the rhythm. Do not play a backing track in your head. The audience/audition panel cannot hear it!

- Minding the structure and creating the overall shape.

  There is no need to snatch breaths, for example, because you are neither leading nor following. Let the physical reflex action inhale the breath for you. Keep focused on the melody, so that you stay in the same key as you move from phrase to phrase. It is always good to have an experienced pair of ears monitoring your interpretation to make sure your version stays within the bounds of good musical taste!

Examples of unaccompanied songs include lullabies, communal song, spirituals, work songs, wartime marching songs, some songs in Shakespeare and of course many folk songs.

Folk Songs

It is very useful to have a selection of folk songs in your repertoire. They can be used for technical study and for auditions. It is also useful to include folk songs from your native country, sung in your native language, or maybe you can choose a song you have grown up with or that connects well with your regional accent. Many folk songs have an implicitly smooth or legato line and they tend not to have too big a range. Because of their simplicity, they are can be quite exposing technically and so they are wonderful tools to show freedom of tone and depth of expression.

We do not wish to write a detailed description of the folk songs that we might include in the suggested repertoire. They are part of an aural tradition of music, being handed down through the ages by someone singing or playing them to someone else. Almost every edition of folk song books contains variations, both in the lyrics and the melodies. We think that it is best that you make your own choices as to how you would like these to be sung and what the song expresses in its story.

Here are just a few traditional folk songs as suggestions to get you started.

The Ash Grove (Llwyn On)
An Eriskay Love Lilt
Greensleeves
She Moved Through the Fair
Scarborough Fair
The Sally Gardens
David of the White Rock (Dafydd Y Garreg Wen)
O Waly Waly (The Water Is Wide)
The Lark in the Clear Air
Fairy Lullaby (Suantrai Si)

These are a few songs from Shakespeare plays, which you should look for in the original settings or traditional versions, and which are often performed unaccompanied.

When That I Was and a Little Tiny Boy (*Twelfth Night*)
The Willow Song (*Othello*)
O Mistress Mine (*Twelfth Night*)
How Should I My True Love Know (*Hamlet*)

18

PRACTISING AND TAKING THE REINS

'Learning takes place at the point of need' – Geoff Bullen, RADA Associate Director and Course Leader for the BA in Acting

Without a 'need', your training will be far less successful. From the self-motivation to learn the words, learn the melody, undertake research wherever appropriate and make creative choices, through to actually taking a breath, this 'need' informs the muscular activity of singing.

'Singing is 90 per cent memory, 10 per cent intelligence, lots of hard work and something in the heart' – Enrico Caruso

Once you begin to experience freedom in your singing, your own practice can become ever more interesting and productive.

Repetition is a vital part of vocal development; as the old Italians said, it takes seven years to make a singer!

'Genius is one per cent inspiration and ninety-nine per cent perspiration' – Thomas Edison

Recent studies such as the 'ten thousand hour rule' have only confirmed what we feel is intuitive – that under the correct set of circumstances, the more you practise, the better you get.

Patience is required, as you may not feel or hear your voice developing week by week. Over time, if you are doing the exercises correctly, the improvement in your voice will become clear.

If you find yourself avoiding practising or looking for reasons not to practise such as mismanagement of time or a tendency to veer towards displacement activities, then you should be aware that this may stem from a psychological element. If this becomes a longer-term issue, try starting with very small objectives in a short time frame to build your confidence through achievement.

Practising

These are some of the things you might like to consider regarding your practice:

* What time of day suits me?

- How frequently should I work?

- Is ten minutes at a time best, or do I need an hour to settle into it?

- Which exercises or thought processes get me into feeling vocally free most efficiently?

- Which are the areas I have discovered that I want to work on most?

It is important to have the self-discipline to avoid overworking areas of your voice that are functioning well just to make you feel better. Remember this is not a performance! The goal is not to sound good to yourself, but to improve the areas of your singing that need work.

You may benefit from setting yourself realistic targets for certain developments, and also for repertoire learning. Be pragmatic. Do a SWOT analysis! In other words, assess the balance of your Strengths, Weaknesses, Opportunities and Threats. Perhaps a weakness in reading music will be balanced by the opportunity offered by considerable free time in which to study!

Singers should develop their own warm-up routine. Warming up is the process of getting into a good place, both physically and mentally to start your practice session. Work with the techniques that you have used in class, which enabled you to feel a greater degree of vocal freedom.

A practice session is different from warming up. You need to bear in mind the amount of time you have to practise, so plan your time accordingly. Make sure you are using your full range each day, to maintain and develop flexibility. A good balance of exercises: fast/slow, high/low, legato/staccato, vowels/consonants, and song singing. Working on sections of your songs can be seen as a technical exercise too.

Gauge how you are feeling each day and accept the fact that you may be physically or vocally tired and that this needs to be taken into consideration. Do not force anything to be what it is not. Make sure you do your practice session when you are able to fully concentrate. Mindlessly bashing away at scales and exercises is highly damaging.

If finding the correct vowels within the words is your weakness, make sure you allow plenty of time to also write down the words phonetically as a visual aid. Diphthongs may be something you need to spend more time on.

When memorising words, you need to develop your own systems which can be refined so that you can achieve greater reliability and efficiency in this area.

Learning songs

A strategy for learning songs needs to be established. Obtain a piano practice track of your songs. You must free yourself from the temptation of listening to another singer's performance of your songs. While a practice track is not absolutely ideal, as you are limited to the feel of a specific recording which does not develop alongside your performance, it is the next best substitute for a rehearsal pianist or coach.

Always learn the words for songs as a separate discipline. It makes your memorising doubly reliable if you do not necessarily associate the words with the tune or rhythm. Whatever targets you have set yourself – learning new repertoire or material for performances, for instance – make sure you give yourself a schedule that is logical.

For instance, start learning songs as soon as possible, so that you can add detail over time. You may be concentrating on music for an audition on Wednesday, but you should also make sure you start work on the song you need to have ready in three weeks' time. Learning songs is a multi-layered process, as described elsewhere in this book, and you will deny yourself the chance to develop your work if you leave working on the process too late.

When is the best time to learn words? While travelling on a train? During the television commercial breaks? You can do something in every circumstance, so look for possibilities to use your time effectively. Very rarely do you have perfect circumstances. A fantasy scenario may be swanning around at home choosing which part of the day to practise and when to relax and recuperate. In fact, within a busy career schedule, you may find that you have to learn your words on trains and planes and practise your breathing and singing in hotel rooms.

Know when to listen to practice tracks, going through the song silently in your head rather than singing all the time. You might want to save your voice by waiting until the information about notes and rhythm is in your head. The voice can tire easily and get you into bad habits if you sing before your brain has everything ready to go. At certain stages it might be wise to sing down the octave if you have particularly high or taxing phrases. Practise at a speed, especially wordy passages, that suits you. The muscles will go slowly from note to note and syllable to syllable to begin with.

Putting everything together can feel like juggling and when practising juggling, one often drops the balls. This should not be regarded as a problem but as part of the process.

Taking the Reins

For your voice to be wholly present and for a song to feel truly alive and nuanced, we feel that you, the actor, must take the reins.

We know that for a student, the words 'experience' and 'confidence' can be quite scary concepts, as by their definition these cannot be obtained quickly or easily. Please see these as cumulative! If you have ever collected anything, you will know that with focus and determination, things gradually accumulate until you feel quite proud of your achievement.

Set yourself some targets – for example, go to a live music performance once a month, stand up and sing in front of someone once a month, watch a DVD of a musical once a month, listen to some music outside your usual interests. At the end of one year, see how much you have learned, how many new experiences you have accumulated.

Take opportunities that are given to you. Every experience is valuable as you begin to develop your sense of judgement and to understand what makes a good performance. This is also your chance to explore repertoire without being chased up about it – or having to deliver a result. Buy anthologies of songs for your voice type.

Find out what your interests are. Explore avenues that pull you well away from your comfort zone. The knowledge of these areas makes the core stronger.

Taking the reins should feel like a positive step. Start making decisions about which repertoire you want to sing or need to sing for particular auditions and performances and which keys are best for you. Begin to be aware which roles are right for you at your stage of development. It is important that you begin to feel empowered to make your own decisions and structures.

However, taking the reins does not mean you have to 'go it alone'. Even when you might be fully fledged as an actor/singer, it is most common to continue to study the art of singing with a coach or a technical teacher. Even if these visits are only from time to time, in the arts we often need the support and inspiration of others to rediscover and reconnect and to continue our journey with added vitality.

19

THE NEXT STEP – WORKSHOPS, MASTERCLASSES, CABARETS, SMALL ROLES

Consider the following five elements as a deconstruction of the whole nature of being an actor/singer.

- Voice
- Bravery
- Theatrical awareness
- Musical awareness
- Self-motivation

These are what you need if you are to become 'match fit'.

Learning to be a professional actor/singer is not just about freeing and conditioning the voice. All of the elements in our list above are crucial to starting and maintaining a career. While it is possible to work on all of these in the relative safety of the singing studio, they cannot be fully explored unless there is some regularity in performing in front of an audience. Building your skills in all areas and strengthening weaknesses will put less of a strain on one particular quality in the list. Being a bit undercooked in any one area is going to really put a strain on the system as a whole.

So once the voice is ready, you should look for a forum which will allow you to start your development as a performer. Clearly, the first step into this world requires a good deal of bravery, but if you are well prepared in the other areas then you can reduce any fear to a manageable amount.

Opportunities where you can feel safe to 'give it a go' without feeling under too much pressure to produce your best performance are really useful at this point. Under these circumstances, you can be brave enough to try out a variety of ideas. You may overbalance the performance in terms of technique or theatricality, but you will definitely learn something! In a supportive environment, feedback from other tutors or peers can be very helpful, or at the very least, thought-provoking.

Attend all sorts of workshops and summer schools and listen to advice and opinions. All of this advice will be useful, but you should ultimately establish your own path. Initially, it can be somewhat frustrating to hear similar comments from different people about your weaknesses, but you should accept these and eventually decide what to do about it. It may be that you agree with what is being said, but you may be resistant if you realize that there is a lot of work to do to improve that aspect. Again be brave! You will need much self-motivation.

You should have a good set of songs, all of which you have studied, some of which you know have been chosen for you for strengthening the voice, some of which you really enjoy or feel are suitable for you. You can gradually increase and alter your repertoire as time goes on. You should be putting the finishing touches to certain songs while beginning to do the background work on others.

Also remember that if you are still in the phase of building your instrument, the songs you will be working on in the background may not be the most appropriate for you to perform. So it is good to hone a set of performing songs and another group of songs to be used for vocal development.

Coaches, directors and colleagues may make suggestions about new repertoire and you should be always on the lookout for new and interesting material. Remember it is often other people that see or hear your potential more easily than you do yourself, and sometimes it is not the music that you enjoy listening to the most that best suits your voice or personality. Make a note of repertoire ideas, perhaps in the back of your diary or on your mobile phone, every time you hear something interesting in workshops, cabarets or performances that you attend.

It may also be time for you to have sessions with a variety of recommended coaches. In the early days of training, it can be confusing to have lots of different influences, but as you become more secure and your technique more robust, it is very interesting to hear a variety of opinions about repertoire and advice about performing styles. Most coaches are involved in a wide range of events and activities, and so they are likely to be a good source of possible chances to perform. They may also recommend you for work or have information about other opportunities or auditions.

Make sure all songs are suitably presented and marked up for your accompanist. It may be that, during the course of a rehearsal or masterclass, a coach or pianist may make helpful suggestions which you can ask them to mark into your copy for reference.

Masterclasses are a useful step, as generally you will have a chance to sing through your whole piece before working on it with an experienced teacher. If nerves prevent you from doing your best first time round, the working session will allow you the chance to relax and have another go in front of your audience. Music schools and drama colleges have developed programmes to allow students the opportunity to sing under these conditions before taking the bigger step onto the concert platform. At RADA we hold an event called 'Verse and Song' which gives our students an opportunity to sing a song and speak a poem in front of an in-house audience. Other group sessions leading up to these presentations operate as a kind of open rehearsal. There are also cabarets, masterclasses and mock-audition classes to build confidence and experience.

The cabaret stage can be a great place to develop your performing skills. The advantage of the cabaret is that to a large extent anything goes; you are afforded the exploration of vocal expression and character which are allowed to be freed from the demands of genre, style, and even those of a musical director. This platform is just a collaboration between singer and pianist and generally takes place in an atmosphere of relaxed intimacy. You are often free to choose the songs that best suit your needs.

If there is no established cabaret easily available to you, then you might have to be proactive in setting up your own. A few like-minded people and a willing pianist is a good start, together with a suitable venue with a piano. The more atmospheric the venue the better, but bear in mind that the most important thing is to make it happen and to have a few supportive people in the audience. Events like this can develop over time. Our cabaret, which takes place in the RADA bar, has grown, thanks to the

Jeremy Legat and Eva Traynor in a cabaret at the RADA bar 2012. Photographer: Linda Carter

great passion and commitment of a group of dedicated people, to become a really great opportunity for artists to showcase their work.

At the beginning of your career, it is very often worthwhile to accept an opportunity to perform a small role for a fringe or mainstream production. As time goes on, you can afford to be fussier about roles you choose to take on, but you can learn much from being in a rehearsal room with more experienced performers. Making professional connections in this way is one of the most useful ways of building a career path.

Ideally an actor/singer will start a career in less vocally taxing parts and progress to the most challenging and most rewarding roles in theatre. Being thrust into the limelight due to youthful strength of voice or seductive good looks can be wonderful, but is also fraught with danger. Pushing the voice to sing big roles before the singer is fully ready can ruin a promising career. Take advice from trusted teachers on what may be suitable for you at each stage of your development.

'There are no small roles, only small actors' – Konstantin Stanislavsky

20
PREPARATION FOR AUDITIONS

In our opinion it is best to delay auditions to gain professional employment until you have attended quite a number of lessons and coaching sessions and feel in control of your process.

The first hurdle in dealing with the audition situation, other than singing well, is having the right song for you that also fits the criteria of your prospective employers.

You are often invited to sing a piece of your choice at audition. Bear the following things in mind when choosing your song:

- While enjoyment of singing should not be precluded in your performance, it is not always the songs that you enjoy the most that serve you the best.

- Choose a song which plays to your vocal and musical strengths, be that a strong top, a well-balanced middle register, a good connection with the text, a flair for comedy, or a particular genre which suits you.

- Do not be tempted to try and display all of your vocal power in the first couple of phrases that you sing. A well-balanced and musical voice may be enough to elicit interest, and if you possess an instrument with power, then keep the forte or fortissimo short and to the point. Keep your songs no longer than two minutes or so. If they cannot be cut down to this length without destroying the form and meaning, consider an alternative.

- Certain songs are particularly challenging to achieve a good ensemble with the pianist. 'Something's Coming' from *West Side Story* is a prime example, where unless the pianist knows the song particularly well, the rhythmic complexity can throw the whole performance off.

- A 'contrasting song' can and should be just that. You do not have to change your voice to achieve this. A change in style, in mood, in tempo, in genre is all that is required. A complete change of vocal timbre can sometimes be confusing to your panel and unless you can do this really convincingly – and not many people can – potential employers may be concerned about your vocal identity.

- Do not focus on the effect that you are having on the panel or indeed on yourself, unless that is inherent in the song.

- Less is More.

Mark any cuts clearly and if you cannot do this yourself, ask your teacher or coach to help you. Any cuts should make tonal and harmonic sense as well as preserving the narrative.

You should be fully hydrated before you enter the room. If you suffer from a dry mouth from nerves, then take a bottle of water in with you and put it on the floor and not on the piano! If this can be avoided, then all the better. After all, you are sometimes on the stage for lengthy periods without having a drink. In addition, water bottles can become a bit like babies' dummies, used as pacifiers during an audition. Try and wean yourself off unnecessary glugging. This may also indicate a nervous personality to your panel.

You need to be wary of having a negative attitude towards auditions. Psychologically, hating auditions gives you a reason to fail.

If you use them, be sure to wear contact lenses rather than glasses, as you need to use your eyes for communication and expression in performance and auditions. It is important to be able to see and properly focus on your audience, or you may find it difficult to focus your voice. Women who know that they will wear high-heeled shoes for an audition, or think that they may be required for a role, should practise in them during the last stages of preparation.

As soon as you get an idea that an audition may happen, it is advisable to start thinking about possible material. Hopefully there will be something from your repertoire that will fit the bill. Often theatre companies keep the song choices for auditions quite general and will simply ask for 'a song', especially if it is part of a more general acting audition or meeting. Sometimes it will be a request for a ballad and an up-tempo song or even just two contrasting songs. Always check the details and check if there is going to be an accompanist present. It can be assumed that there will be an accompanist for Musical Theatre auditions, but that may not be the case for an acting audition, so you or your agent need to be clear on this point.

Unless you are auditioning at the highest level for Musical Theatre, accompanists will vary in their capacity to play complicated accompaniments at sight and unless you are very lucky, there is almost never an opportunity to go through the music with the accompanist first. It is therefore usually sensible to choose a song, or a version of a song, that has a reasonably straightforward accompaniment. Your coach will be able to tell you what is suitable.

At the time of writing, it seems to be common practice to turn up at acting and Musical Theatre auditions with photocopies of songs. The main reason is that, providing you put your song into a folder or stick it together with sticky tape, the page turns are easier for your audition accompanist. Talk to your coach about the most appropriate way of presenting your music. It is important that you have photo-copied directly from your own book or have legally downloaded it from a reputable music supplier on the internet. Always take the original score in your bag as well as your photocopy.

Take the sheet music in the key you are intending to sing it. It is completely unreasonable to expect an accompanist not only to sight-play, but simultaneously transpose your piece into another key. Do not go to an audition with a backing track. This is not karaoke!

The choice of material is important. It should show off your voice and give the opportunity for you to embody characterisation. If you have enough time between the initial information about an audition and the audition itself, you can do some research into suitable material for the particular style of music that will eventually be performed. If you are auditioning for a particular character, try to find a song that has similar qualities, or a similar style, perhaps in humour, genre, age or emotional thrust. If the style is laid-back or energetic, go for something similar. If the character is quite subdued or extrovert, try to find this quality in a song. It is always better to sing something that you have already performed. As the panel may have strong ideas about the way in which a character will be played and sung in their production, it is generally not a good idea to sing a song from the show you are auditioning for unless you are particularly requested to do so.

Sometimes the breakdown – audition guidelines – will be very detailed and sometimes you will even be asked to sing a particular song or a song by the same composer. If it is more general, you need to quite quickly research suitable songs and make decisions as to whether these are achievable both technically and interpretatively in the time allowed. It may be that the project you are auditioning for has provided information that you should be abreast of, so that you can enter into an informed conversation with the audition panel.

Hopefully by the time you are attending high-level auditions, you will have a fair knowledge of styles, genres and songs. Maybe you will have bought a few volumes of songs, perhaps a few vocal selection volumes and some anthologies of pieces that are suitable for your voice type. If you cannot find anything suitable, ask your coach or singing teacher or a trusted colleague.

It is always a mistake, unless absolutely necessary, to learn something in a hurry. If there is time, try to get a singing lesson or coaching session before the audition, particularly if you are going to sing something new. If not, do not rush into singing the song through. Make sure you do the usual preparatory exercises. There are so many pitfalls: memorising reliably, having enough time to rehearse with a pianist, preparing the score properly, getting the song 'into your voice' and developing an interpretation. This is why it is important to build up a good repertoire while you are in training and then to keep adding to it.

If you do have to sing something that is not perfectly prepared – perhaps the audition is at short notice and a particular song has been asked for – then take other songs that you know well to use as additional material should they ask for it.

Think through your days leading up to the audition:

- Make sure there is nothing unnecessary in your schedule.
- Can you make time for more practice?
- Can you make time for more sleep?
- Can you avoid using your voice too much, especially the day before the audition?
- What will you wear? Ideally you will want something comfortable which might also make you feel and look a bit more like your character.
- Find out where the audition is, make travel arrangements and work out how much time you will need to get there.

Avoid leaving preparation until the last minute and think through what else may be asked of you or what you may be asked to do in the audition.

On the day of the audition, keep your schedule very organized. Have your meals, clothes, transport all planned and if possible avoid stressful situations before the audition. If you have any other personal strategies for managing stress, utilize them now!

You will need to make sure you have warmed up on the day. Unless you know that there will be a space at the audition venue, it is best to do the bulk of it before you leave home. You can be humming as you walk down the road, reading through your words on the train. Sometimes you have to do some last-minute warming up in the cloakroom at the venue! This can be a bit intimidating if there are other singers around, but it is important that you give yourself the best chance when you walk into the audition space.

Always have, for any audition, a prepared unaccompanied song in reserve. Quite often in an audition for a straight play you will find yourself being asked: 'Could you sing a bit of a song?' Be prepared. Also, it is invaluable to have an unaccompanied song up your sleeve for the day when you turn up to the audition room to find that there is no pianist – for whatever reason.

Be prepared to introduce the song you will sing with the correct and full names of both composer and lyricist. Never introduce a song by saying: 'Cry Me a River by Billie Holiday.' Arthur Hamilton would not be happy! Be prepared to answer questions about the song you have chosen to audition with, about the piece it comes from, the character that sings it, and more importantly, be open to any suggestions or adjustment that the musical director or director may ask of you in the room.

Sometimes you will be asked for the range of your voice or voice type. There are two elements to this:

- Know your voice type. This is normally dictated by your comfortable average pitch area (known as vocal tessitura) – this defines whether you are soprano, mezzo soprano, contralto, tenor, baritone or bass.

- Range – this is more absolute and defines your upper and lower limits of pitch.

Take a folder of other songs that you feel confident singing into the audition room. It is quite common that an audition panel will ask for a choice of material, or when they meet you may change their minds about how they would cast you, so they may wish to choose a more suitable song from your folder.

Make sure you have eaten, preferably an hour or two before the audition itself, and keep hydrated.

Do not enter the audition space carrying anything more than you need. Hopefully any excess possessions can be left somewhere safe outside the room, or if not, put them down immediately at the side of the room. Walk into the audition room as yourself. Be as prepared as you can be and deliver your song with confidence. Do not second-guess what the panel might want, but be true to your artistry and sing with integrity and belief.

The accompanist will usually ask you for the speed of the song (tempo) and if there are any cuts. Hopefully the cuts will just need to be pointed out on the music that has already been marked up. It is a good idea to sing the first phrase or a phrase in the middle that has, for example, more notes in it. This may offer a better indication of the right speed for your interpretation. Sing gently but confidently, not under your breath, as this may result in a tempo that is incorrect.

Stand close enough to the piano and make sure that the pianist can get at least a side view of you, so that they can properly accompany you. If you make a mistake, or something goes wrong, you need to be able to see each other.

Eye focus while singing your song is often a question we are asked about. You may get a feeling for what is appropriate in the room. Use your imagination to create, focus on and interact with other characters, perhaps the person to whom you are telling your story. Focusing on the panel is not normally recommended. You need to give the panel the opportunity to observe you rather than making them feel part of the performance. If you are in any doubt about what is wanted, ask the panel for guidance.

At some point you may audition for new musicals, or plays with new music. These may be difficult to find suitable songs for and you may find that people want to explore some of this new material with you in the audition room. Do not be afraid to ask the same questions of the panel that you would ask yourself in preparation. Who is the character, what is the situation, where are they? Even a little information can help you begin to interpret the character.

Always thank your accompanist when you collect your music and leave the room.

Experience is often the key to being confident in auditions. Your first few attempts can often be quite stressful and nerve-wracking. In any case, be realistic – you may have sung well, but not be what the panel is looking for. It is always a good idea to think through each audition after the event, assessing

what went well and where you need to improve. Consider carefully whether you chose the right repertoire. Regard any feedback that comes your way as a welcome bonus. It is tempting to put the whole
experience out of your mind, especially if it did not go well, but if you can think through the process
logically, it should help with your next audition.

21
REHEARSALS AND PERFORMANCES

Rehearsal Technique

Idina Menzel and Kristin Chenoweth rehearsal footage of 'For Good' from _Wicked_ by Steven Schwartz – DVD extra segment, from PBS documentary, Broadway the American Musical, 2003
Two leading singers of contemporary American Musical Theatre in the early stages of rehearsal. Notice the collaborative nature of the rehearsal, the positive creative energy, and the sense of exploration in the expression of the music. Menzel can be seen feeling the rhythm and exploring how any vocal coloratura might add to her expression. She seems quite unperturbed when she feels that she might have missed a beat!

Elaine Stritch – 'The Ladies who Lunch' from _Company_ by Stephen Sondheim – film of the rehearsal for the original cast recording, Columbia 1970
An insight into the tension that can build when creating art. Elaine Stritch's line, 'It's breaking my heart but not my spirit', is a valuable lesson!

So, you've got the job. Congratulations!

It is important to consider ways of managing yourself through a rehearsal process when you are a member of a company preparing a musical or theatre piece with singing.

There will usually be a covering letter with any material that you have been sent in advance. It may be that you need a 'working knowledge' of the music and script by the time of the first rehearsal.

Sometimes for a smaller company where rehearsal time is shorter, it may be that you need to be 'off the book', in other words to have learned everything from memory. Whatever it says, be prepared.

You should have done as much research and technical preparation as possible, and have developed a genuine engagement with the piece. Usually you would have read the whole play, script or libretto.

Generally speaking, the better your vocal technique, the more equipped you will be to thrive in the rehearsal situation. Any unnecessary tensions or false supports for your vocal tone will greatly hinder the development of your role. As previously mentioned, the balance of resonance in your vocal tone should be flexible, and although every voice has a tonal fingerprint of sorts, the impact of action, intention and character will and should have a profound effect on your sound.

Often you will have individual singing coachings before the rehearsal process starts, so that your knowledge of a role is as advanced as possible. With a smaller company, the onus may be on you to get your own coaching on a role and certainly some singing lessons before you arrive at your first day of rehearsal. However, it is important that you do not fix on an interpretation or a style of delivery. You can offer these, but you need to take on the creative vision of the overall shape of the piece. It is very probable that your character will change and develop hugely within the rehearsal process, and you need to be flexible and open to everything that is offered. Nevertheless it is very important to maintain vocal health and safety at every point. Your singing voice is a musical instrument and its alignment must not be disturbed. This is your responsibility, and even if you are being asked for extreme vocal use such as screaming, you must get that scream from a place of technical awareness. In the rehearsal room no one but you is looking after your voice and your technical process. Indeed, you are the only one who can do it.

Even if you have a musical director looking after you, you must take responsibility for your own vocal integrity all the way through the rehearsal process. There is no time to fuss about your vocal condition (perhaps you have a cold) in the rehearsal room. Any residual problems or ongoing issues need to be sorted out in your own private time. Rehearsal time will be spent in developing your character as part of the company as a whole and if something about the production is not working for you vocally or feels uncomfortable, you can always try to resolve these in collaboration with the director or musical director. Most directors will welcome ideas if they will help to develop and realize the overall vision.

The vocal workload on an actor rehearsing a musical or singing within a play is often very taxing, both physically and psychologically. Each role will have its own specific vocal demands, but as long as these demands are compatible with your instrument, the voice will become conditioned to a particular tessitura (average pitch range) and vocal quality during the rehearsal process. This is known as 'singing the role into the voice'. Just as an athlete conditions him or herself for a particular event and the body adapts to its specific demands, so the voice will adapt and respond physically to the rehearsal process to become more appropriately fine-tuned to the demands of the vocal score. As you would imagine, the analogy does not end there. Likewise, recovery is all-important for this process to properly occur. The more muscular stress that occurs in the physical activity, the greater the time required for rest and rebuilding. Diet also plays an important role in this process and the correct nutrients and hydration are vital if the voice is to flourish.

Avoid pushing or driving the voice for effect in rehearsal and see dramatic climaxes as the equivalent to athletic sprinting. Sustaining this high-intensity work will cause the most muscle fatigue and, if not done technically well, will very soon send the voice into decline. Substituting clarity of intention for volume is especially useful in rehearsal to avoid vocal tiredness. In a bigger role, plenty of vocal rest will be necessary during the rehearsal period to maintain good vocal health and to build vocal stamina.

Avoid spending too long in noisy places such as the pub and try and get plenty of sleep. Some actors like to make sure their diet is supporting them by supplementing with vitamins, for example, during the most physically stressful period in the run-up to opening night. Keeping your carbohydrate level sufficiently high is vital. Eat complex carbohydrates to avoid sugar spikes and their corresponding lows. These can be dangerous for the voice, as the body can lose vitality and the voice can be damaged quite quickly, and this will in turn start to create psychological strain. Enough protein needs to be taken on board to keep the body repairing itself, and enough vegetables and fruit and salad to keep general health robust and the immune system fully operational.

The rehearsal room can become quite a harbour for viruses, especially towards the end of an intense rehearsal period when some actors and technicians are a bit run-down. Try to avoid instant energy hits of sugar and caffeine which are no substitute for a good healthy dietary regime. This might all be a bit too much for some, but even if it seems quite a small cog in the overall mechanism it might for some be the cog that allows the whole system to work.

Ensure that you have a bottle of water with you in rehearsal, especially in the theatre and when rehearsing under lights, which can be drying for the throat. When rehearsing in your own clothes, be comfortably dressed for movement and wear layers of thin clothes so you can be better equipped to adjust your body temperature if the space is too hot or too cold.

Be a good colleague and company member, supportive of others and their process but equally protective of yourself, so that you do not waste energy. Be generous. Be aware that any negative attitude to your work or anybody else's can be highly addictive, so be really wary not to develop this pattern. Equally be careful not to pick up other people's negativity.

Saving your voice or marking

It may be necessary, in prolonged rehearsals or if your voice is suffering from an illness, to save your voice from vocal strain. To 'save' effectively, it is important to keep your general energy level high but to use less energy in and around the larynx itself. You may consider 'marking', which is singing the high passages for your voice down the octave, or even speaking those passages in the rhythm of the music. Singing the high passages at the correct pitch in a soft tone can lead to a lack of vitality and can actually be harmful for your voice.

When repeating a scene over and over, the focus may not be your vocal tone, so judge how much voice you need to give in each repetition. It may not be necessary to fully sing out your top note each time. As long as you have tried it and you feel it is there, then it may serve you better to save it for later in the rehearsal process. Do speak to the director and the musical director and establish that if you need to save, that this is indeed acceptable, and ensure that this does not impact negatively on the rehearsal process both for you and for others. It is very common for the leading singers to save their voices in the rehearsals leading up to opening night. Technical rehearsals are normally very long and tiring for the actors, and to sing your bigger scenes repeatedly while the lights are moved around is not generally necessary.

There are other elements to consider in the transfer from the rehearsal studio to the stage. The acoustic may be very different and there will be issues of adjustment – particularly if you will be using microphones, which may make you hear your sound quite differently.

Before the Show

Allow time for your warm-up but be careful not to overdo it. If you are engaging in a company warm-up, embrace the process but we recommend that you do your own vocalising before this occurs. Be at the theatre in plenty of time and allow yourself some quiet time as well as time for any physical or mental preparation that you find helpful. In addition, there will be all the usual demands – receiving production notes, checking props and so on. If you find that general chatting in the dressing room is tiring, distract yourself by focusing on your make-up or even by more mundane activities such as doing a crossword.

Singing is good for the spirit. Amidst the tumultuous drama school schedule this half-hour oasis gives a student time to reflect on their journey so far, perhaps work on their confidence, and sing out their hopes and fears. They say that the emotions in Shakespeare are carried through the vowels. Singing releases these texts beautifully by connecting the breath, voice and deep emotions. For a theatre actor one of your primary concerns is that your voice will stay healthy during a long run. Voice coaches will often ask actors to sing a few lines of their text during the warm-up for a show. It frees the voice and the imagination, and you can really sense your voice soaring to the back of the auditorium through song.

Bryony Hannah – RADA Graduate

The Performance – Break a Leg!

Brett Brown in *Poppy* by Monty Norman and Peter Nichols: RADA Production 2008. Photographer: Mick Hurdus

Considering the title of our book, you might expect a whole chapter on performance, but from our experience and that of our many students, in the performance itself, you must trust your preparation and your rehearsal process and be in the moment vocally, totally free to express yourself.

Sometimes performers find that the performance situation brings a particular type of concentrated focus which uniquely takes their characterisation and technique onto a new level, and which only occurs when performing.

RADA graduate Henry Goodman as Tevye in the West End production of *Fiddler on the Roof* by Henry Block, Sheldon Harnick and Joseph Stein, produced by Kim Poster for Stanhope Productions at the Savoy Theatre, London 2007. Photographer: Catherine Ashmore

After the Show

This is a time for slowly warming down before going to bed and resting for the next day's vocal exertions. Have something light to eat and drink to replenish your reserves but try not to go anywhere noisy if you are eating out and do not prolong your socialising any more than you need to, as the voice will need a good rest to fully recover. Make time to think back over the performance and take on board any lessons learned.

Early in your career, it can be difficult to find a balance between the thrills and spills of working in the performing arts and the responsibility of serving the work. Remember that, au fond, it is a job like any other and you have a duty to the art and to the audience. As Kipling put it, 'If you can meet with triumph and disaster and treat those two imposters just the same', you will be well on the way to finding that balance!

22
TROUBLESHOOTING

Good singing technique should be such that problems do not arise frequently.

The solution to many problems with your singing can be found in the fundamental principles of posture and breathing. Imbalance and problems with breaks in the voice often occur when the voice has been subject to abuse or strain. If this becomes a problem, you should return your focus to basic technique. Sometimes you may have to take some time out from performing until the voice has found its natural balance once more.

Using different accents or vocal characteristics when singing can upset the balance of the instrument if not done correctly, and the voice will need to be conditioned back to its more natural state before embarking upon the next acting task.

It is often wise to go back to the beginning and analyse the components of the singing mechanism as you did in the first few lessons. Hum, speak, sing the phrases of a song on the vowels of the words, and so forth. Maybe you will find one component that is out of place. Maybe if you look in a mirror, you will find that your posture is incorrect, that your chin is jutting forwards or you may be singing with your mouth too closed or too open. Fundamental principles are your first port of call to troubleshoot a problem.

Nerves

If you suffer from nerves, do your best to stay true to your technical process. For many performers it seems that the positive aspects of nervous energy outweigh the negative. To try and hide or deny your nerves may compromise your aspiration to be free in spirit to perform without artifice.

At RADA we move incrementally through a series of events during which students gain an understanding of how nervous energy might affect their voice. Group sessions, masterclasses, rehearsals and presentations are a precursor to any sort of formal performance. Occasionally the students say at these early events that everything tightened, that their knees shook, that they couldn't breathe freely, even that they couldn't remember what happened during the actual event! It is quite common that although the student felt these symptoms quite severely, listeners, and sometimes even the teacher, were unaware that the student was experiencing this level of anxiety and the physical symptoms that go along with it.

By the time our students are asked to sing a song to their whole year group, their new technical skills are, for the most part, strong enough to counter the effects of their nerves. As singers ourselves, we realize that a great deal of bravery is needed in these situations. We regard these presentations as an exercise, rather than a performance, so that the emphasis is on what might be learned as opposed to achieving success or failure. We give support and feedback to students and, following these events, we go straight back into the work to develop what has been discovered.

Clavicular breathing

This is a common fault during the in breath and often occurs when there is a fundamental change in posture in order to try and fill the lungs with air as a conscious process. This results in lifting the upper chest and clavicles from their optimum postural state, only for them to be lowered again on the onset of tone. This process prevents the diaphragm from properly engaging with the breath and throws the balance of the voice away from a centred core colour. Clavicular breathing can be caused through habitual misuse or by fear or panic in the singer, brought on by a negative or judgemental attitude. This misuse must be overcome if the student is to realize their potential.

Illness

When you are sick, rest the voice and body as much as possible. If necessary, find out from your doctor exactly what the problem is as soon as you can. Sleep is often a good way to get over common colds and so forth.

If you have a head cold, it is often quite easy to sing, but if you have a sore throat, or worse still an inflamed larynx (laryngitis), you need to be very careful and take advice, especially if you are involved in performances. If you decide to go ahead, be very careful to keep the health of your singing voice at the centre of your performance – this is when you need your technique the most.

Air conditioning and aircraft pressurisation

These environments can be very dehydrating. Ensure that you drink enough water.

Nasality

This can be caused by tension in the jaw, tongue, soft palate, or by an incorrect mental approach as to where the notes are placed in the head. This sometimes occurs if you are listening too much to your own sound, perhaps stemming from insecurity about staying in tune. If this condition persists after working on your core techniques, medical advice should be sought.

Catarrh

It is easy to say, but the best thing is to try not to cough or clear your throat. Try sipping warm or room temperature water. In severe or persistent cases you might have to investigate possible allergies or intolerances. This condition may be alleviated by inhaling steam.

Vocal strain

This is usually caused by lack of balance in the vocal system. Some of the direct reasons for vocal strain can be as follows:

- Singing the wrong repertoire.

- Singing in the wrong tessitura.

- Belting without good technique.

- Shouting.

- Working or speaking in a noisy environment.

- Smoking.

- Clubbing or talking over music.

- Excessive football supporting!

- Stress.

- Lack of basic technical understanding.

- Overworking.

- Oversinging.

- Tension.

Wobble

The most common cause for this is pushing the voice to make it something that it is not. The effect of this is that a natural vibrato becomes slow and uncontrollable. A singer needs to work systematically and with a good degree of patience to turn around this condition.

Diphthongs

Inappropriate execution of diphthongs can be quite destructive and can cause tension. Sometimes a singer will tend to sustain the wrong vowel when singing a diphthong because the correct vowel is difficult to sustain vocally. This obviously needs addressing by attending to fundamental techniques.

Glottal attack

Be careful not to start a vowel with a forceful coming together of the vocal folds. This is termed a glottal attack and is often detrimental to vocal health. To remedy this you can practise putting an 'h' in front of the vowel to get the breath moving and eventually use a silent 'h'. There are various exercises in our book which address this issue, for example in many of the sections in the chapter Ways we Work with Actors. Unlike speech – because in singing you often have a different note on each syllable – you can afford to ally consonants to vowels, where in speech you may need a cleaner attack. This more fluid and musical approach to diction should eliminate the need for glottal attack or glottal stops as they are sometime known.

Wordy phrases

If you are singing a passage or a song with fast words, sometimes known as a patter song, be careful not to over-articulate or try to spit the words out to 'play the effect'. This often causes tension in the throat and can destroy the balance of the core colour of the voice, making the words harder to discern. Keep the vocal line fluid and attend to basic technique in order to address this issue.

Ensemble

If you are singing in an ensemble, it may be that you feel the voice starts to tire more than it usually does when singing on your own. This is because the vibrations and sounds of other people's voices around you confuse your sensory mechanism. It may be that you sing entirely differently under these circumstances. It is more imperative than ever to have done your own warm-up before you sing with a group. Also choral or ensemble vocal tessituras cause trouble for certain voices. Often tenors and sopranos have to sustain quite a high vocal tessitura, while baritones and mezzo sopranos have to maintain a low one, rather than use more of their range as they would do during solo singing. Be sure you have experienced all of the components of your own singing process before embarking on a group activity. This will strengthen your perception of yourself within the group and help you to maintain good practice.

Tone deafness

It is hugely rare that someone otherwise in good health cannot match any pitch to a voice of similar range and quality. It is much more common that a student might have problems with singing in tune or with wandering off the melody. These issues often stem from a lack of confidence to sing, or sometimes from a voice that is balanced a long way from its natural core colour. It is our experience that when students with tuning problems begin to think more positively and begin to regain greater balance and physical ease in their voice, that melody begins to flow in a much more accurate and sustained manner.

Our approach is often to home in on a note that a student is comfortable singing, and we match pitch with them, rather than expect them to do it with us. Once confidence in one note has been established, then we encourage the student to move to a note higher or lower than it and back again, and so forth. Even if the progress is slower, we use exactly the same principles as set out before, to begin to develop the capabilities of each vocal instrument. Helping students with these issues is probably one of the most satisfying teaching and learning experiences for us as teachers.

Common Pitfalls

These are some of the common pitfalls that we have encountered and we strongly advise that you avoid the following:

- Singing along to recordings. You can easily lose your identity and you certainly cannot reliably learn or memorize your song by this method. Would you learn a speech by speaking along to a recording?

- Singing along to exercise tapes with earphones in. It distorts the perception and 'feel' of your voice and can be very confusing.

- Comparing your progress to other students or other singers in a negative way – you cannot hear your own sound properly anyway. You have employed your teacher to be your analytical ears. You need to allow progress to happen at your own pace. As long as you are committed to the process and working hard, natural development will happen. The speed of progress varies hugely, and interestingly it is quite rare that the voice sounds better and better week by week. Often a voice can sound pretty well the same for several weeks, but because a student has worked very hard, a big leap of progress can sometimes seem to come out of the blue. It is also not uncommon for there to have been apparent vocal 'settling' when a student arrives back at the studio after a short break.

- Listening to recordings of yourself as value judgements when you are in a developmental part of your training. A voice can develop with sudden growth spurts in different areas, and so may be out of balance for some of the time while it is in training.

- Having long gaps between singing lessons, especially early in the training. You need a teacher to keep you on track. If you make mistakes, they need to be corrected before they lead to bigger vocal issues.

- Leaving long gaps between practice sessions and then trying to do everything in one long session. As with any other discipline or sport, practice needs to be regular.

- Not practising because you think you have misunderstood. Do it anyway! Your teacher will reset your work accordingly.

- Trying to reinterpret how a teacher is teaching you – they have a reason for saying 'focus on communicating over a long distance'. If you notice at that point that your support is much stronger, for example, then do not say to yourself next time 'support better' – stick with the original instruction until the elements of your technique become inextricably linked and you feel like the integration of the elements of technique have become natural to you.

- Practising in a non-conducive environment where you are fearful of making sound or where there is distracting background noise. An acoustic that is too resonant can also be inappropriate.

23
MISCELLANY

This chapter is written to be a bite-size reduction of concepts and important words discussed elsewhere in the book. Some other ideas or words appear here for the first time. It is not a glossary of singing terms, and is not intended to be comprehensive.

Arpeggio

Literally 'harp-like'. A musical pattern of the first, third, fifth and sometimes eighth degree of the scale is a staple diet of many exercise regimes and is known as a major (or minor) arpeggio, depending on the 'flavour' of the third. This can also be extended up or down in the same manner.

Articulation

'About the outer gate my lips and jaw and tongue shall play with all the supple freedom of a graceful dance; and bring to life the beauties of my native speech.' – W. A. Aikin

There is hidden depth in this phrase that reveals itself the more the training and understanding of singing progresses. The words play, life, supple, freedom, graceful, beauties, native, all have considerable resonance in the process of developing articulation and are chosen in this phrase with such specificity and ease. Specific problems with functional articulation are really the remit of a speech teacher. In terms of the singing voice, over-articulation can be just as bad as under-articulation – the problems caused merely being of a different kind.

Authenticity and the natural voice

Once an authentic speech quality has been discovered and recognized by the student, it is imperative that this quality is nurtured and that singing becomes an extension of this form of self-expression. Singing does not sound the same as speaking, but the tonal fingerprint of the natural speaking voice should be present at some level in all ranges of the sung tone. Ironically this is the hardest adjustment to make on your own and perhaps requires the highest expertise from the teacher to sense when the voice is authentic and natural to a particular student. The singer lucky enough to have discovered their own sound early in life will typically have fewer vocal problems and may therefore be technically more advanced even though they have not had any lessons. For these lucky natural singers, entering the world of vocal instruction can be dangerous. Good, natural singing may come about through a combination of factors. Perhaps being exposed to and emulating freely expressive tone from an early age is the key.

In the words of Stephen Sondheim: 'Careful the things you say, Children will listen, Careful the things you do, Children will see and learn.'

Belt voice

The belt quality was presumably first arrived at by a wonderful singer/actor who happened upon this sound as a result of total technical control, coupled with expressing an extreme emotion in the moment. It has become a way of communicating something musically and theatrically in a heightened state. Belting is an extreme vocal state, and in this book we do not attempt to teach you how to belt, because without a teacher to advise you personally and monitor your progress, you may put your vocal health in jeopardy.

Much has been written about belt. At its best it can be a thrilling theatrical effect and at its worst it can lead to the destruction of a promising voice. It can be likened to the sprint at the end of a race and a worryingly common error in seeking this effect too early can be likened to a person sprinting when they have no basic fitness, little understanding of racing tactics or crumbling joints!

It is interesting to note that the hugely successful coaches of British Cycling are committed to developing talented young cyclists as all-round skilful and fit riders, before attempting to work on the powerful sprint aspect needed by the next crop of potential Olympic medallists. Likewise pointe work in ballet is never embarked upon until there is enough strength and flexibility to sustain this physically. As with all muscular activities, some people are more genetically suited to activity requiring endurance and some more to activity requiring speed and power. When belting, it is absolutely imperative to stay true to sound principles of basic technique, as the most common problem in this area, which to a certain extent is magnified by the industry itself, results from competitive belting, which is the beginning of the end!

Suppleness in the body and vocal tract should be established before attempting a belted tone. Jessie J is a superb example of this, her throat being extraordinarily supple and her body able to move as she wishes when singing fabulous belted tones.

It is fundamentally wrong to sing high notes as dramatic notes before they can be sung lyrically. Belted tone need not destroy the voice if it is properly understood and, crucially, used sparingly. It is in its simplest form a musical use of a calling vocal quality. A higher throat energy is used in belt and it always pays in this demanding type of singing to keep the body and mind alive and in the moment. Extra care needs to be taken to ensure that basic technique is always adhered to, as any technical flaws when belting will result in very quick deterioration of vocal condition. As with other elements of technique, responding to musical and theatrical demands is critical, and making tone as an 'end product' is not in line with being free as an artist.

Belting has different implications for the female and male voice. Errors occur in the female voice when not enough head resonance is present as the voice rises in the middle register and the voice sounds unmusical, laboured, heavy and shouty. This prevents the register shift which is the key to accessing high belt – up to top F and higher. In this case the natural mechanism of thinning the vocal folds for the rising note is not being allowed to occur, and instead the vocal folds may become too thick.

In the male voice it is debatable whether there is a need to belt at all, in that a well-produced forte in the upper register has just as much power as a belt tone, need not be operatic or inherently old-fashioned, and can be achieved with much less tension. Belting in the male voice is essentially not making natural adjustments in the throat that create tonal adjustment in the top register but instead extending a fixed concept of vocal tone to the top of the range.

The development of the voice cannot and must not be rushed. The pressure on young singers to belt in order to achieve employment and for schools of singing to produce the most impressive singers can lead to the promotion of speed over thoroughness. The appropriate amount of time must be allowed so that every singer in training can achieve balance and freedom when their voices are ready.

It is only when female students can successfully manage the middle register of their voice, and when there is generally a good physical and mental understanding of technique, that songs that demand a belt are looked at. When commercial aspects of singing do not impose so much upon our students, this often has genuinely beneficial aspects for developing a good technique.

Best of Shirley Bassey – BBC TV programme, 2013
A superb compilation and an hour well spent. Incredible insight into how great technique and impeccable musical taste will allow an extraordinary singer to develop throughout their life. For singers interested in the belt quality, the climax of 'I Am What I Am' at 40 minutes is well worth listening to.

Idina Menzel/Tracie Thoms – 'Take Me or Leave Me' from *Rent* by Jonathan Larson – 2005 film
This is a good example of contemporary belt and of great ensemble music-making. This quality of vocal tone is exhilarating at its best but needs to be executed really skilfully to avoid vocal strain and damage. Even fine exponents of this style can suffer vocal problems if this amount of laryngeal energy is sustained for too long.

Franco Corelli – 'A Te, O Cara' from *I Puritani* by Bellini and Pepoli – EMI recording 1961
Franco Corelli had technical expertise that allowed him to exploit his natural dramatic instrument to the full. The top of his voice had incredible strength right into the autumn of his performing career and he is proof that singing dramatically need not compromise vocal longevity as long as the technical foundation is correct. His top demonstrates that men need not belt in order to sing dramatic high notes and brings into question whether they should be considered in a different light at all. His ability to diminuendo from forte at the top of his voice is legendary.

Belting, an alternative viewpoint

In an interview given by the R&B singer Beverley Knight, she expressed that she never considered that her tone had a belt quality. For her, the word *belt* had physical and psychological connotations that she was very unhappy with as a performer. She explained that her singing education came from her church and that her voice should be never less than beautiful in the eyes of God, while a belt had indulgent qualities that distorted her natural singing gift. Perhaps this is a modern way of expressing the old saying that singing should be 'never louder than lovely', though perhaps it should say 'never louder than natural' or even 'never less than truthful'.

Gospel church singing is just one of many early life experiences which may contribute greatly to creating a free instinctive response, and has undoubtedly had a profound effect on the evolution of vocal tone used so extensively in modern American Musical Theatre.

Cadence

Taken from 'cadere', meaning to fall. In music, a cadence is where a musical phrase comes to a complete or incomplete close. It does not necessarily have to *fall* in order to do this, so this is a now a bit of a misnomer stemming from very early music. It is important not to drop the energy at a cadence but to manage 'every cadence with fullness of tone', to quote W. A. Aikin.

Choral singing

Training for the actor/singer should include some choral singing. When approached correctly, this discipline is not only highly enjoyable – as is much collaborative art – but can really help in the development of musicianship. If you engage in a good balance of choral singing and solo work then poor technique that may occur, when sight-reading for example, need not hinder vocal progress. Care must be taken not to spend too much time in this discipline as often the vocal tessitura of a harmony line is taxing for the voice in some way. Singing as part of a first-class ensemble can be a truly inspiring and creative activity and can open pathways to deeper musical expression in the individual.

Coloratura

Italian for 'colouring', the word coloratura is used in singing to describe passages of notes sung on one vowel at speed. It is important to include this study in your daily vocal workout in order to develop a supple and flexible vocal tract. If done correctly, the ability to sing faster will improve with practice. Singing fast notes can also be the key to extending the range upwards, as top notes should be sung as short notes before they are sustained. Using musically haphazard patterns in scale or arpeggio-like passages can often inspire greater vocal freedom than more musically organized vocalisation, which can make a lot of students tense, attempting to 'get it right'. This is a great way of finding more freedom and technical accuracy in scale singing and coloratura. Return to tonality once this freedom of attack has been discovered.

Dynamics

Dynamics, or gradation of loudness and softness, add a great deal to vocal performance. They are a product of an imaginative and creative theatrical process. Solo singers do not really employ dynamics in the same way as choral singers where the conductor is in charge of the overall tonal effect. Attempting dynamics can often lead to pushing or pressing for loud sound or being vocally undone trying to sing too softly before the voice is sufficiently coordinated to do so correctly. For the advanced singer, precise control of dynamics is a powerful tool for nuanced vocal expression.

Emotion

'Much of interpretation comes from the courage to leave words alone. Words are beautiful in themselves' – William Shakespeare (the singing teacher)

The beginner should not overly concern themselves with emotion in song. Very often it is their own emotion in the process of learning how to sing that is preventing them from learning as well as they might. In a more intermediate stage, the student has to take care not to force the emotion in an artificial way, as this can lead to a quality of general emotionality. In the exposition of the melody of a song, the advanced singer should focus on freedom of function and let the words ride on an authentically 'open' tone. This can be quite a magical and genuinely artistic form of expression.

There is normally a place in a song where it pays to show exactly how you are feeling in a more visceral and demonstrative way in that moment. An advanced singer will sense where this place is and will make this the climax. This vocal climax will be all the more effective if the quality associated with it is not overused. Emotion induced by the imagination need not destroy vocal technique but as an interesting effect it can momentarily change the normality of singing tone. This is a special effect and must be used sparingly.

The Steinway Analogy: Consider the world's leading concert pianists, how they are able to express a range of profound emotions from great joy to deep sorrow, while the Steinway piano remains constant, balanced by great instrument builders. It is in the mind of the performer that the emotion is born, stimulated by the musical composition and informed by the player's life experience and imagination. While the audience can be deeply moved, experiencing a wonderful emotional journey, the instrument has remained unchanged by the emotional experience of the player. The tone of the Steinway remains resolutely well balanced and is not undone by emotionality.

Singing is not quite like this, the voice being organic and capable of assuming a huge variety of colours and timbres. This can very often be a problem in itself in the communication of real feelings and can prevent the natural range of expression and gesture, both external and in the vocal tract itself. In short, the voice should not be consciously coloured to achieve an emotional effect but the tone should be consciously monitored to remain true and authentic.

Falsetto

While the falsetto is used by the counter tenor to achieve their specific voice, the same quality may be used by the male actor/singer as a special effect. The particular techniques required to fully develop the counter tenor voice are not relevant in this book. Some high sopranos have a flute register very high up in the voice which some believe is the equivalent to the male falsetto.

Alfred Deller – Feste's song 'With a Hey Ho the Wind and the Rain' from *Twelfth Night* by William Shakespeare, traditional

The counter tenor voice was popular in music of the medieval and baroque periods, but then suffered a decline. Alfred Deller is credited with reintroducing this voice type during the first half of the twentieth century, through the sheer beauty of his tone, clarity of words and effortless range. As well as singing early music such as this traditional Shakespeare setting, Deller also worked with composers such as Benjamin Britten and Michael Tippett on new repertoire. Contemporary counter tenors such as Andreas Scholl have extended the classical repertoire, while in other genres, singers such as Freddie Mercury, Martin Jacques and Klaus Nomi have taken the voice into new areas.

Habituation

This is a word that describes the way in which we learn new physical tasks, from walking and talking as infants to playing a Rachmaninov piano concerto. Habituation is what happens when we repeat a task so often that what at first seems clumsy and hard work eventually becomes a smooth-flowing and effortless operation. This is sometimes referred to as muscle memory.

Iconic performances

Do be inspired by iconic performers and do aspire to achieving iconic performances, but keep your feet on the ground and realize that these performances were not arrived at overnight and were likely to have been the result of years of training or experience and the reaction to a sophisticated collaborative artistic process. Focus on your own process and set short, medium and long-term goals for your progress.

Imagination

'Singing is hopeless without imagination' – Harry Plunket Greene

Wise words which sum up perfectly the importance of an integrated approach to singing. To metaphorically leave 'yourself', or your imagination, in the wings of the stage or – worse still and more commonly – outside the singing studio, is to make a fundamental error in approach. Nicholas Barter, a former Principal of RADA, once told a year group who had just sung on stage to 'Keep your star shining, both in class as well as in performance'.

Internet video sites

At its best, the internet is an invaluable resource for twenty-first-century students. There are many truly inspiring clips of international artists singing at their best, masterclasses with internationally renowned teachers and vocal experts talking eloquently and with much insight about their craft. The flip side, and the worry, is that with the ability to instantly summon up performances of just about any song, a karaoke style of singing is being promoted, with 'performances' being arrived at before the student is ready.

Legato

The smooth transition from one note to another. This is not exactly a slide, but a slide done so elegantly, quickly and efficiently that it appears that the notes are not linked at all in this manner. A good legato is essential in good singing and a crucial tool to both vocal longevity and communicative lyrical singing.

Memorising

'But I know this song!'

Memorising by singing along with a recording of your favourite artist in the vast majority of cases does not work! You will be relying on aural cues for your vocal entries and for the text and this is not a reliable or recommended method.

Find your own method of memorising but include writing the words out and speaking them with intention. Sing the song in your full voice, sometimes with a piano backing track, so that you can work on the melody and rhythm of the piece. This is not a substitute for having a coaching session with an accompanist but is an acceptable aid in the learning process. There are many songbooks which now include backing tracks and there are web sites that also provide this service. You should be able to do several speed runs of your song without error before you declare that you know your song!

Messa di voce

Literally 'putting the voice' or voice placement. This was an advanced exercise used in the bel canto school where crescendo and diminuendo were practised daily. It should only be employed by the advanced student and should be first explored in the easiest range of the voice before extending the exercise to upper notes. It is interesting that the voice placement should be considered not to be forward or back, up or down, but be the ability to make a crescendo and diminuendo. One of the most famous exponents of this effect is the Italian tenor, Franco Corelli.

Methods and books

Plato said that music and gymnastics were the basis of an ideal education. The process of intellectualising singing, while it may be interesting, is not for the most part necessary. The issue with a method-centred approach to teaching and learning singing is that it disenfranchises students whose learning styles do not suit it.

The difficulty in writing a book on singing is that the real skill of teaching it is not only assessing what the individual student needs, but also knowing how to present the content of this work so that it affects the desired change in the student in the moment. This is the 'art of teaching' and is not the main subject of this book.

We feel strongly that it can be counterproductive to inform students of the physical details of their vocal progress moment by moment as this can prevent creative energy being used to unlock tensions. When vocal balance and freedom can be sensed and felt, then the student can and should be made fully aware of the physical process that has enabled this to happen. This is simply best practice. To inform a student what an exercise is for before they do it increases expectation and more often than not decreases effectiveness. This is not best practice.

This is why books can be misleading, and why their value is only as an aid to a course of study, not as a substitute.

Mezza voce

Mezza voce literally means 'half voice' in Italian and should not be confused with *messa di voce*, which means putting or placing the voice. Mezza voce is an advanced effect where the volume is greatly reduced while the central core tone remains steadfast and well supported. Attempting to do this before the voice is sufficiently coordinated can lead to problems. Done well, the floating quality that can be made in mezza voce is very descriptive and emotionally engaging. It can also be used as a kind of musical stage whisper.

Mixed voice

Mixed voice is a very useful concept for the actor/singer because it is one that refers to the mixing of resonance as a natural effect throughout the voice. We work intensively on the middle register and expect the natural quality of tone here to always be a mix of head and chest resonance. All notes in the voice except perhaps the extremes should be more or less mixed like this.

'Every note is a mixed note' – Viktor Fuchs (student of Jean de Reszke)

This phrase may have been taken from a bel canto idea referred to as 'voce mista'. This was used to describe the tone quality used when high tenors of the bel canto school sang notes in their upper range without greatly increasing laryngeal energy by pushing, and also without resorting to a falsetto quality.

Exploring another inference of the term, it can be a device used to address the imbalance of resonance as the contemporary female belt quality rises in pitch and loses the benefits of head resonance. In this case it can be seen as a way to bring lyricism and greater ease and accessible range to the modern-day belter.

Mixed or mix voice and belt voice for these singers should be thought of as related to each other, so that the one never seems so far from the other as to prevent meaningful expression. Another benefit of this is that employing mix can help to avoid vocal tiredness from the build-up of pressure and energy in the larynx associated with belt. Some singers can discover that their 'mixed' tone becomes almost as strong as a belted tone, so this can be quite liberating. As we see it, mixed voice describes what occurs when the instruction to speak in your home area, and to do nothing more than this with your speaking element, combining this with the concept of moving the notes in your head, elicits a tonal balance in terms of resonance, and will be part of good singing as a natural effect.

The musical score

Discussing his music, the composer Gustav Mahler would say that everything was in the score – except what was truly essential.

Study your music well. Do not paraphrase. Observe musical dynamics and, where appropriate, stick to general principles of style. As with all rules, it often pays to bend or break them! As Mahler so brilliantly put it, an accurate musician can also be a truly bland one, but a performance without accuracy cannot be fully fledged. Work hard on musical accuracy so that the rhythm and notes become second nature. There is no freedom without discipline. You cannot be truly free and in the moment unless you have done sufficient work to unlock what the composer and lyricist have written down on paper.

Opera

Opera is a theatrical art form where singers and instrumentalists perform a dramatic work, combining text and music. The earliest Dramma Per Musica on stage was developed in Italy and was some time later called Opera, the plural of opus, which simply means 'a work'. Audiences often went solely to see and hear the stars of the day and when their favourite singer was not on stage, indulged in various diversions to entertain themselves.

Grand Opera usually refers to large-scale nineteenth-century works with substantial choruses, large orchestra and many actor/supernumeraries and dancers. These productions were possible because apart from the stars in the leading roles, instrumentalists, singers and actors were paid very little and so impresarios vied with each other to present the greatest spectacle.

Contemporary opera often explores challenging modern subject material such as the first visit of a US president to China, *Nixon in China*, or the writings of the neurologist Oliver Sacks, *The Man Who Mistook His Wife for a Hat*, and pushes the boundaries of musical expression in the same way that writers such as Sarah Kane, Martin Crimp and Anthony Neilson have explored extreme possibilities in theatre.

Much work is currently being done to break down the boundaries between Opera and Musical Theatre. In our opinion this can only be a good thing and there is no reason why a contemporary audience should not enjoy *Peter Grimes* as much as *Parade* or, indeed, *The Magic Flute* as much as *Sunday in the Park with George*. The film version of *Les Misérables* may be a case in point, and is a fantastic foray into the fusion of European Grand Opera, Contemporary Musicial Theatre sensibility and Hollywood blockbuster!

Projection

'And all my countrymen will hear me and understand' – W. A. Aikin

A quote that is both simple and aspirational. You must be clearly audible, but if in striving to be heard you compromise the audience's understanding of the text, then you may be pushing and will need more technical work on your instrument. Pushing or driving the voice can also be a telltale sign that there is insufficient investment in the appropriate level of storytelling in your song. Systematic conditioning of your instrument will in time make issues of under-projection much less of a problem. Attempting to speed up this process can often make matters worse. Take care when attempting to spit the words out. Often, over-articulation can compound the effects of unnecessary tensions.

Cerca la qualità, e la quantità verrà
– an old Italian adage roughly translated as: look for the quality and quantity will come.

Range

All singers want to work on their vocal range. We all have our natural limits – there are sopranos, mezzo sopranos, contraltos, tenors, baritones and basses. These are generalized, as there are various subdivisions of these categories and the compartmentalisation is actually more fluid. There is also an overlap regarding vocal quality and range; some sopranos can sing lower than contraltos and some baritones have a high B flat! The categories are more reflective of comfortable tessitura, or average range, rather than the highest or lowest note that can be well sung. Having a big range is highly desirable as it can open up the choice of songs available to study and perform, and can offer the promise of more dramatic repertoire. Focus on singing with your own voice and not singing like a baritone, or like a mezzo soprano, or like any category of singer. This is one of the factors that often result in vocal dysfunction regarding range. There is a natural temptation for the student to push the process of range building and the thoroughness of technical study can become distorted into a quest for ever higher notes. Often the reason why a high note has not been well sung is that the note or notes preceding it were badly produced. The same may apply to notes at the bottom of your range. Range will be increased as technical work gives you more control over vocal bridges and the balance of resonance becomes more natural in the middle range of the voice.

Using an emotional quality for high notes as a substitute for technical control can be exciting, but it is not sufficiently thorough to serve the student in the long term.

Recitative and aria

A precursor to verse and chorus in terms of musical form, the recitative and aria was an invention that made the development of through-composed opera more possible. In recitative there is much more emphasis on storytelling, with the text and the words generally moving much faster. It is where the plot is advanced between the songs. In the aria (literally meaning air or melody) the storytelling is a more musical affair and musical rhythm tends to dominate.

Historically recitative was separated into categories, which included 'secco' or dry, which was only accompanied by a harpsichord and a cello (also called the continuo) or 'accompagnato', which was accompanied by the orchestra. Recitative accompagnato was a halfway house between full-blown melody singing and a kind of musical speech. These forms are still prevalent in contemporary compositions, as a whole opera made up entirely of arias could extend to many hours. Wagner was the composer that took this idea to extremes, with his operas lasting well past closing time!

Recitative accompagnato and arioso, a close relative of this, are very popular with contemporary American Musical Theatre composers such as Jason Robert Brown.

Repertoire

Your current, known songs are known collectively as your repertoire. Be pragmatic about the way that you choose songs to increase your repertoire. Consider the function of any new piece that you wish to add. Is it a song which will help with long-term vocal development? An audition piece which suits your voice and casting? Or a song that you like to sing? Working on inappropriate material for the desired outcome can make technical progress really difficult and can lead to vocal problems. Songs that you most like to sing could be quite inappropriate for your long-term development, and while it may be fine to sing these for you own enjoyment, you must be realistic about your developmental needs. Another common mistake worth mentioning is neglecting the finest songs in their genre because they are currently too popular! While it is probably best not to take a really popular song to an audition, these pieces are popular for a reason and you can often learn much more about singing from a well-crafted song than a lesser piece.

Resonance

Resonance is the scientific phenomenon of sympathetic vibration occurring in the chest, mouth, sinus and nasal cavities and also to a lesser degree in the skull and bones themselves. It is to distort the concept to attempt to create resonance as a primary effect. The colouring of the voice and the subsequent change in the balance of resonance brought about by the imagination need not disturb the vocal technique and the instrument can maintain a musically satisfying complexity. Colouring the voice by direct muscular manipulation can simplify this function, resulting in a less than satisfactory tonal palette and a lack of nuance in performance.

Thinking more deeply, consider the philosophy that what is resonating is in fact the deeply felt emotion or deeply held belief that underlies the particular notes and words of a song, and it is this emotional core that the resonance is surely amplifying.

Rhythm and word stress

A good sense of rhythm is integral to free, expressive musicality. Rhythm is inherent, quite literally at the core of our being. Our heart has a beat which changes with our mood. Problems with rhythm can often stem from fear and self-doubt.

The general rule for word stress is that when the expression is head-led, then conversational rhythms govern the text. Alternatively, when the expression becomes heart-led, then musical stress pattern and rhythm take over. An example of this is that higher notes may seem stressed despite the function of the word within the sentence. Exaggerated equal stress normally infers a heightened emotionality, as also does a musical triplet (three equally stressed notes) which is a musical indicator of this. Compare a child who is in control of his emotions telling a parent that he is 'not going over there' with the same scenario where the emotional child issues forth that he is '*Not Going Over There!*'. This must be understood in order to make sense of word setting in music and can resolve many examples of seemingly poor setting of words, especially at vocal climaxes where musical stress is clearly placed on the wrong part of the word or the sentence. This is likely to indicate that the level of emotion has rendered normality redundant and the surge of the music is completely in charge. Singers should be wary of using exaggerated equal word stress at the beginning of a song, demonstrating a generalized heightened emotionality and thereby leaving less scope for the emotional journey of the character through the piece. Singers should always observe the fluid passage of words in good speech and seek to emulate them in song.

Rubato

A technique associated with rhythm. Stemming from the Italian word for 'robbing', to use rubato is to pull the speed of the song around, to slow down and speed up in order to increase the expression of the music and the text. Care needs to be taken not to be overindulgent with the use of rubato and a useful guideline is to keep the march of the song steady – where there has been a slowing down there should often be a subsequent speeding up. Think of it as a well-managed bank account. You can take out as long as you put back in!

Scale

A stepwise movement up or down through the pitch range. There are many types of scale, with many different musical 'flavours' or 'colours'. In western music, the major and minor scales dominate.

Slur

An exaggerated, slowed-down legato joining two different pitches by an audible glide. While sometimes useful as a vocal exercise, it is also used to good musical effect if utilized sparingly and tastefully to give certain musical phrases a more communicative and emotional quality.

Soft Palate

The soft palate is situated behind the hard palate at the back of the roof of the mouth. It should not be consciously controlled as this has an effect on its natural position and vibrancy depending on the demands of pitch and timbre. The soft palate moves as a natural result of changing pitch and timbre. Common errors in the use of the soft palate are holding it high and stiff in a yawn position or dropping it, creating fixed nasal tone. Creating a supple and reactive soft palate has a knock-on effect on the entire vocal tract and can often be a hugely remedial tool for unnecessary tension in singing. Jaw tension can often stem from soft palate and associated laryngeal tension.

Squillo

The Italians used the term squillo to describe a high, ringing tone, sitting or floating on top of the voice. If you return to the head hum exercise described earlier on page 40 in the chapter, Ways we Work with Actors, it is possible to explore how this tone is made.

In the exercise you began by 'trapping' a vibration – made by humming a note in an easy part of your vocal range – in a small box inside your head. The most common feeling is that the box is somewhere behind the nose – there isn't a particular place where this is right or wrong and it is interesting to play with moving the box forward and back by small degrees with the power of thought, while at the same time getting a feel for the change in vocal tone. So, we sing from somewhere behind the nose, not into, or worse still, down the nose, but in fact in any direction outwards.

Pushing this box as far forward as it can go is a little like forcing yourself to the very front of the stage. Being a little further back from this is the optimum place to achieve a squillo quality. Think of it as the icing on the cake. To artificially find this high resonance by pushing the voice forward can be very destructive, as any type of forcing or pushing distorts the natural or authentic centred quality which is the key to truthful expression and natural vocal gesture. The icing makes the cake taste much better, but you would not consider serving it on its own.

Stephen Sondheim

'Where would we be without Sondheim?' – Darell Moulton

Our highly esteemed senior tutor in singing at RADA expressing our debt of gratitude to the body of work by the great American composer, which is a profound influence in the development of our students. Perhaps more connected in his work to Purcell, Britten and certainly Ravel and Tchaikovsky than the American theatrical greats, his work is unique and inspirational. He is a towering figure in contemporary musical and theatrical writing for the stage. Geoff Bullen, the Course Leader for the BA in Acting at RADA, once said that just as we speak of 'Shakespearean England', history might have it that we are living in 'Sondheimian Times'! Sondheim is in many ways a true pioneer but we believe his work also connects deeply and remains true to the earliest aspirations for a totally integrated form of Dramma Per Musica, where words and music emanate equally from the centre of our very being.

'Anything you do, let it come from you, then it will be new' – Stephen Sondheim, from *Sunday in the Park with George*

Style
A very important element to the successful performance of a song, the style or authorial voice of a song can in some cases be the key to unlocking expression. Care must be taken, however, that particularly strong styles do not upstage the content of your song and the authenticity of your sound. Some styles of singing have developed alongside a lack of technical expertise and studying too much of certain repertoire can have a detrimental effect on the development of the voice. It is easier for a singer who has had a good training to make a 'bad sound' than a badly trained singer to make a 'good sound'. Becoming entrenched in a single style is not helpful for the versatile actor/singer.

Technique
Technique should be regarded as a means to an end. Technique should be centred on bringing the student to their authentic tone. In the study of singing, musical, poetic and theatrical aspects of voice must also be developed, and neglecting one of these crucial areas of study will almost certainly have negative effects on the voice. Developing the voice as an instrument is a process of naturalisation by repetitive correct functionality, and while the needs of composers, lyricists and musical directors should be borne in mind, an authentic and freely imaginative and individual response to material should be the focus.

Tessitura
Tessitura is an Italian term which describes the average pitch range of a song. A song may not have any high notes, but a high tessitura can make it feel as though it was written for a high voice. As an actor you are often asked for your vocal range, and while this is important, it is equally important to be

aware of the tessitura of a role, as the highest and lowest notes are not always an accurate indication of how the writing will feel in your voice. As your training progresses, you will become more aware of the vocal tessitura that best suits your voice, a little like discovering which athletic event best suits your physicality.

Training

'You cannot improve nature, but you can allow it to develop. You can allow nature to work naturally, but there is no improvement of nature' – William Shakespeare (the singing teacher).

To fear vocal training because you think that your natural gifts are going to be compromised is to completely misunderstand the purpose of what training should be, which is not to be moulded into the person desired by a teacher, an institution or an industry, but to be developed physically, psychologically and artistically so that your full potential can be realized.

Transformation into character

This can be a real tonic for many voices in training. Where a block in creating free vocal tone is psychological, character work can be a magic key to unlocking the singing instrument. Vocal tone produced by an imaginative, transformative impulse is generally energized and often free from self-judgement and many of the exercises used for exploring and developing the singing voice stem from this idea. Transformative games are especially good as warm-ups, working to connect mind and body.

Certain actors seem to reveal more of their potential to sing when they feel that they are being someone else. The most fortunate have the ability to transform and maintain authenticity. This is to be celebrated, and sometimes actors that were at first reluctant to sing find that deferring the responsibility of singing to their character diminishes their fear, making their innate talent more evident.

Trill

A vocal trill is a fast transition from one note to another and back or an oscillation in the muscles of the larynx. It is not a musical effect that occurs often in musical scores written with the actor/singer in mind, although there are plenty of examples in the Musical Theatre repertoire – 'Green Finch and Linnet Bird' from *Sweeney Todd* being one of the most obvious. In this repertoire, it is an effect used more by the soprano voice than the others, but all voices should practise this effect as a building block in vocal technique as it promotes flexibility.

Vibrato

The small oscillation in pitch that occurs as a natural effect of freely produced vocal tone. The human voice is the only instrument that produces vibrato as a natural effect – other instruments manufacture the vibrato in the sound where it is needed to convey feeling. Vibrato will start to emerge as the voice develops and should not be forced or faked – this would be known and heard as a wobble.

Voice clinics

The British Voice Association (BVA) is a supportive network for students, and has a very helpful database on its website, which lists voice clinics and specialists all over the country, who can help you with vocal health issues.

Voice types

In classical voice training, and in the world of classical singing, voices are divided into categories dependent on timbre or tonal colour and tessitura or comfortable average pitch range. For the female voice, the broad categories (from highest to lowest) are soprano, mezzo soprano and contralto and for the male voice they are counter tenor (the highest male voice using the falsetto quality), tenor, baritone, bass baritone and bass. In Opera, there are many subdivisions related to the roles the singer is likely to perform and the particular abilities of their instrument. Examples of these include dramatic soprano, lyric tenor, Verdi baritone, basso cantante. The complete list is very long and gives an insight into how singers are cast very specifically in this genre.

The particular qualities that place a singer into one of these subdivisions may not be obvious at all at the start of the training and a particular type of voice should not be seen as a target. As mentioned elsewhere in this book, to try to sing like a Rossini tenor, rather than focus on the process that gives you your own vocal freedom, is almost always counterproductive.

As an actor/singer, the matching of specific roles with voice types is much more fluid, although the same issues of vocal tessitura need to be considered when deciding whether a role is suitable for your voice. Just because you can sing the highest note required by the score does not mean to say that you can comfortably negotiate the whole role. Average pitch range needs to be considered and it may well be that this sits too high or too low for your instrument. The dramatic nature of the writing also needs to be taken into account. It may be that the songs in the role are too physically demanding for your voice type. It is interesting that in classical music (and in general community singing) men will sing an octave lower than women. It is not always the case that this places the song in the same register of each respective voice. Women's voices generally are not a whole octave above men's voices, so singing at an octave apart will often place the female voice in a relatively higher tessitura than the male voice. In contemporary Musical Theatre, composers often prefer to have men singing a little higher than their comfortable pitch range and women a little lower so that they can sing in the same octave or harmonize in thirds or sixths to naturalize this effect. This can create issues for male singers where they have to push their voices up in range to sing their roles, while for female singers it can create greater difficulty with the bridging area in the middle of the voice.

It may be interesting to note that although male and female voices may be singing in different octaves, the pitch at which the accompaniment is played will be the same, regardless of who is singing.

Vowels

A vowel is the part of the word that carries the majority of vocal tone in singing as well as the pitch necessary for melody and lyricism. As the pitch range becomes higher, often as a result of an increase of emotion implied in the text, conversational quality defers to exclamatory or musical tone. As a result of this, songs with a higher tessitura have a more instrumental nature and can be more difficult for the actor/singer to unlock. The idea of vowels and not words can be helpful in the adjustment needed for the correct working of the upper part of the vocal range in song. This can be a most rewarding area of study for the more advanced actor/singer.

Warming up

Warming up need not be a protracted and arduous business but instead a gentle flexing of muscles to get the blood flowing and the mind tuned in and focused for the task which lies ahead. The better the vocal technique the less warming up should be necessary. It is a good idea to clear the mind of negative thoughts in the warm-up period and to focus on technical work that is pertinent to your particular stage of vocal development. Warming up can include a variety of vocalisation, conversational speech, declamatory speech, phrases from songs, vocal glides and so on, as well as conventional musical exercises.

'Exercises are like razors' – Edward Brooks

What Edward meant was that repeating reams of badly produced vocal tone does not constitute a good warm-up or good practice. Warm-ups should be centred on obtaining the sensation of a well-produced sound.

CONCLUSION

We hope that the joy of communicating the sensation of good singing has emerged from these pages and that our book will provide encouragement and inspiration to a future generation of actor/singers. If there is one thought that we would most like to leave you with, it is that singing is simply tuned, sustained speech. Although in singing the tonal aesthetic may be anything but a spoken one, as an actor, it is imperative that you speak to us!

Edward Brooks once wryly observed that by the time you really discover the truth about vocal freedom it's probably too late! As the recording of Harry Plunket Greene shows, age is no barrier to communication through song. We entirely agree with Edward and Lyndon, and with all the other teachers who have inspired us, that as a singer we are always on a journey.

If just one idea that we have offered from our journey – as students, singers and teachers – has helped you in any aspect of your work, then we will feel truly rewarded.

We wish you the best of luck and urge you to enjoy each step of your journey. Whatever your path may be, we hope that what you have read here has been of interest to you and will help you to develop your Singing on Stage.

As when speaking, with singing you simply need to tell the story. Learning to sing at RADA was the beginning of a personal journey to open up my voice and therefore myself to the world around me. It has helped me to feel at home with who I am and exposed me to a world of joy which I have cherished ever since.

Jennifer Kidd – RADA Graduate

Ella Fitzgerald – 'Cry Me a River' by Arthur Hamilton – Verve Records 1961
This is a very good example of how Ella seems to speak to us absolutely authentically and effortlessly while at the same time playing her voice as though it were an extraordinary jazz instrument. Truly breathtaking in its communication and depth of expression.

Frank Sinatra – 'You Make Me Feel So Young' by Joseph Myrow and Mack Gordon – Songs for Swingin' Lovers, Capitol Records 1956

The young Sinatra. Enjoy!

CODA

Jane

I had no thoughts of being a singing teacher until I was unexpectedly catapulted into the role in my teens!

I had started singing lessons at the age of four, following in the footsteps of my brother Tommy. He had been taking lessons with the local teacher Elizabeth Henson, and singing in concerts – a mix of the 'classics' and 'songs from the shows' – as much to help with his asthma as for his enjoyment of it. Just for fun my mother took me along too. Like so many of the most influential people in my life, Miss Henson introduced me to her subject against a backdrop of other interests which all came together in support of the joy of making music and singing. Reading, baking, gardening and painting with oils were her other passions, and over the piano in my music room I have her painting of the garden, where she attempted to teach me about flowers and butterflies, while the aroma of freshly baked and perfectly moist chocolate cake hung tantalisingly in the air. (I never did get that recipe!)

This idyllic part of my life came to an abrupt and tragic end when she died suddenly, when I was sixteen. I was asked by some of her younger students if I would help them with their songs for the festival that they were preparing for, and so we worked together, as we all felt that this would have been what Miss Henson wanted. I discovered quickly that I was very comfortable indeed working with songs and with students one-to-one. It was a source of personal fulfilment to be able to help. The enormous debt of gratitude I have to Miss Henson is immeasurable and she had unwittingly set me on a path that has been a large and rewarding part of my life.

Continuing my studies with Agnes McPate – an equally enthusiastic baker and lover of life – I auditioned for and was accepted by the Royal College of Music. I had been a bit of a star in Peterborough, winning all the competitions – a big fish in a small pond – and for the first six months my path as a student at the RCM was alarmingly rocky, as I desperately tried to be as good as everyone else there. Looking back now, my teacher, who was an international concert singer, did not seem to be able to spot this flaw in me.

After six months I discovered my teacher was leaving due to an increasingly busy concert schedule, and I was transferred to Edward Brooks. Fifteen minutes into our first lesson I had found a vocal freedom and re-established a joyful connection with music. It was so simple. Over thirty years later, I still work with Edward when I have a new role to learn and want an opinion I completely trust.

I do not have any regrets about my difficult moments in the first couple of terms at the RCM. As Edward helped me rediscover my authentic self, I learned much about correcting vocal issues which I have used in my teaching ever since. Further inspiration came from Lyndon van der Pump's lectures on The Art of Teaching Singing. (Thanks to him here too for furnishing us with the information about the history of singing at RADA.) Alastair Graham was a wonderful coach and there were many others. In the

RCM Chamber Choir with Sir David Willcocks I learned more about meticulous musicianship than I had ever known was possible. It was a small miracle.

On my first Friday at the RCM, I had met the woman who was going to be one of the most influential people in my musical life. Else Mayer-Lismann taught Opera Appreciation. We were to become very great friends, though at first she seemed to regard me as a bit of a challenge, and made me painfully aware how little I knew, positively scaring me into running round London attending every concert and opera performance possible.

Else was a Jewish refugee who had arrived in England just before the onset of World War II. Her mother had been the official lecturer of the Salzburg Festival, and they had rubbed shoulders with the likes of Richard Strauss and Clemens Krauss. Else had studied singing with Adele Kern, whose recordings I adored, and she had sat in on rehearsals and performances of all the 'Greats'.

At the end of class one day, Else 'informed' me that I was to become her new stage manager and props organizer for the Opera Workshop! And from then on I spent my Thursday evenings and Saturdays in a church hall just off Kensington High Street. At the Mayer-Lismann Opera Workshop, a small group of students was drilled in all the aspects of opera through working on scenes, with studies in movement, language coaching, Wagnerian gesture, acting and, interestingly, two hours of Tai Chi per week which I was allowed to join in. There was wonderful coaching from Barry Jobling, Anthony Negus and others.

Observing Else and her incredibly talented and insightful assistant Jeanne Henny, I noted the care they took to nurture each individual and the skill with which they drew out each student's musical and dramatic possibilities, while at the same time displaying huge regard for the work itself – the operas of Mozart, Wagner, Verdi and others who Else described as her 'gods'.

To reward my work as a stage manager, when I graduated from the RCM, Else and Jeanne gave me a scholarship to join the Workshop as a fully fledged singer. I was in heaven.

I began professional concert work as a soloist, and to sing small roles with touring opera companies. Colleagues and directors and conductors encouraged and mentored my understanding of singing on stage – too many to number, but particular thanks to my very good friends, Sarah, Mark, Philip, Colin, Jonathan, Elaine, Kevin, Tim, John, David, Chris, Andrew, Jenny, Leon, Philip, Richard, Nick. These are people with whom I share my itinerant career as an opera singer – to date, over sixty roles in over fifty operas for more than twenty opera companies throughout the UK and around the world.

I started teaching at RADA around the same time as I began my singing career. Maintaining both halves of my musical life has sometimes been a delicate balancing act, but it has been a great joy to have them operating simultaneously and feeding each other.

On arrival at RADA I discovered an environment in which all of the teachers felt equal and supportive of each other, and I have learned so much from so many colleagues. It is invidious to single out individuals, but I want to mention our two former Principals, Oliver Neville and Nicholas Barter, and our current Director Edward Kemp. The late Robert Palmer was a guide in my early years. Sue Cowen and Helen Strange were passionate colleagues and remain friends. Other longstanding colleagues and friends – Pat, Lloyd, April, Geoff, Mike, Sally, Nona, Andrew, Robert, Howard, Francine, Jo, Katya, Darren, David – continue to be inspirations. In the singing team it is a privilege to work alongside Darell, Frances, Tom, Jonathan and of course Phil, and to have had as former colleagues Beth, Meryl and Andrew, as well as the late Craig Barbour who is much missed.

My work abroad as a teacher has brought me into contact with Susan in Oregon, Tim in Sydney and Tatiana in Moscow. I am grateful to Albert and Bruce, the clowns, for their input into our book, and to Alli, Mark, Chris and Katya for reading it through in draft and for offering their wise words and thoughts.

Thanks too to Ian and Nick for their skill and generosity in helping with the musical examples and illustrations. Also Rosy, Alli and Mkisa for their loving care and for helping with so many administrative tasks. I am grateful to the whole of my extended family, especially my sons – Matthew for his incredible patience and for his cool typing and graphics skills and Daniel for listening and for his unwavering support and bright ideas.

Both Philip and I are humbled that so many distinguished graduates – students of all the teachers in our team – have contributed their thoughts about the importance of their RADA singing lessons.

I would like to thank all of my students past and present, and everyone who has allowed me to share my ideas with them. I have learned something from each and every one.

My late mother and father – Win and John – gave me all the opportunities that I needed for a life in singing. I feel very lucky and immensely grateful to them that I have been able to make my living entirely by making music.

Last but by no means least, it has been a pleasure to share the process of writing this book with my co-author Phil. We have helped each other to tease out our shared beliefs and there has been much laughter along the way.

Philip

In formulating these thoughts I have learnt that in regard to my musical and theatrical influences I have been truly blessed! Lists like this are impossible, but mention must be made of the following people:

Peter Boorman – Organist and Choirmaster of St David's Cathedral and my first singing teacher. He was the first to show me how to *think* notes and not *do* them.

Sir Nicholas Jackson, who succeeded Peter at St David's and who became a major musical influence on me from a very early age.

All my Choirmasters during my time as a Treble at the Royal School of Church Music, and notably Sir David Willcocks, Lionel Dakers, Martin Howe and Michael Fleming. These important choral conductors introduced me to the special feeling of being involved in world-class ensemble singing. Sir David was the first to open my eyes to the importance of rhythm and Martin Howe and Michael Fleming in particular inspired a sense of 'musical' feeling from deep inside me.

My first rehearsal with the National Youth Choir still feels like yesterday! The inspiration that I felt in that moment stays with me and continues to inform my work. Michael Brewer showed me a sense of musical rhythm I never knew existed.

Martin Hodson – a fine Welsh tenor and all-round gifted musician. Without Martin's teaching I would not have been able to follow my chosen career path.

Even as quite an elderly man Gerald Davies' voice seemed so young and his vigour, stamina and technique was an inspiration. Gerald was my teacher for a year and his Italian sound was important in the early development of my adult voice.

Jeanette Masocchi – a fine coach and teacher who helped me through my vocal pubescence.

Adrian Farmer and Numa Lebin. Numa was a Russian bass and his influence on me was none the less profound. He taught me to think for myself, and without him I would certainly not have gone to the Royal College of Music. My formative years at Nimbus Records changed my life. Adrian was my coach at Nimbus and is the current Director. His playing inspired in me a level of musical and theatrical engagement in combination that I had hitherto not experienced.

My influences at the RCM are of course too many to list. Fellow students and teachers provided inspiration as a daily backdrop to my six years there in full-time study.

My piano teacher at the College and later my vocal coach, Alastair Graham remains the most creative accompanist that I have had the privilege to sing with. His tonal palette was staggering and through his playing he introduced me to the idea that a piano could indeed sing.

Lyndon van der Pump and Edward Brooks were my two singing teachers at the RCM. Their influence on me as a singer and musician cannot be easily put in words. I have always assumed that they are aware, having had similar guidance from their teachers, how much of a debt of gratitude can be felt by a singer to someone that can show you how to free your voice. With me in particular, they showed me the most precious of gifts that any teacher can possess – patience!

I would like to thank all my esteemed colleagues at the Webber Douglas Academy for their knowledge, help and support during my time at this most special of drama schools, and the Principal, Raphael Jago for letting me get on with what I did and make mistakes along the way. I greatly miss the special familial atmosphere that pervaded 'Webber D'.

Having taught at RADA for twenty-five years, you can imagine the list of influences that has informed my work to date! The Principals that I have worked for, Oliver Neville, Nicolas Barter and Edward Kemp have always been supportive on many levels, not least creatively, and my colleagues have shown me ways of working at the leading edge of the industry. Working with a generation of students, among whom are to be found the finest acting talents in the English-speaking world, has not only made my work more rewarding, but has informed it at its core and continues to do so.

I would like to thank my wife Christine and my children Anastasia and William for taking care of things when I was putting this book together, and for generally putting up with my inability to multi-task at any acceptable level.

Through her own teaching (she's still at it as passionately as ever) and her attitude to life, my mother Marion has instilled in me the importance of seeing everybody as an equal. Of course her unconditional love is immeasurable in its depth. I cannot thank her in words for these gifts.

Lastly, not only do I owe who I am to my late father David, but in addition, his undying passion for the finest music-making (and his bewildering eclectic taste), allied to an almost constant playing of it at home on his latest hi-fi, kindled in me, even as an infant, a desire to create it myself and inspire it in others. It is this desire that has been the overwhelming force in my professional life.

BIBLIOGRAPHY

24 Italian Songs and Arias (1894). G. Schirmer Inc., reprinted New York 1948.

Aikin, W. A. (1910, new edn 1951), *The Voice, an introduction to practical Phonology*, rev. H. St John Rumsey. London: Longmans.

Assersohn, Ian (2008), *First Time Bars – A Choral Singer's Handbook*. Surrey: Apple Tree Music.

Baldy, Colin (2010), *The Student Voice*. Edinburgh: Dunedin Academic Press.

Finch, Alfred Ashfield (1942), *A Study of Caccini's Le Nuove Musiche*, M.Mus Thesis, Eastman School of Music.

Fuchs, Viktor (1985), *The Art of Singing and Voice Technique*. London: John Calder Publishers.

Garcia, Manuel (1894), *Hints on Singing*. Aschenberg: Hopwood and Green Ltd.

Hines, Jerome (1982), *Great Singers on Great Singing*. New York: Doubleday and Co. Inc.

The Hundred Best Short Songs (Volumes 1–4) (1930), selected by Elena Gerhardt, Sir George Henschel, J. Francis Harford. London: Paterson's Publications Ltd.

'An Interview with Mr. William Shakespeare', *The Musical Herald and Tonic Sol-Fa Reporter*, ed. J. C. Curwen, March 1891.

Manen, Lucie (1987), *Bel Canto*. Oxford, New York: Oxford University Press.

Palisca, Claude V. (1989), *The Florentine Camerata: Documentary Studies and Translations*. Music Theory Translation Series. New Haven and London: Yale University Press.

Pleasants, Henry (1967), *The Great Singers*. London: Victor Gollancz Ltd, Macmillan Publishers Ltd. 1983.

Plunket Green, Harry (1912), *Interpretation in Song*. New York: Macmillan.

Ristad, Eloise (1982), *A Soprano on Her Head*. Moab, UT: Real People Press.

Salaman, Esther (1990), *Unlocking Your Voice: Freedom to Sing*. Chicago: Trafalgar Square Publishing.

Shakespeare, William (1898–1899), *The Art of Singing*. London: Cramer.

'The Society of English Singers', *The Musical Times*, Vol. 57, No. 881 (1 July 1916), pp. 319–24.

Turner, J. Clifford, rev. Morrison, Malcolm (1987), *Voice and Speech in the Theatre*. London: A & C Black.

Voice (1983), in *Yehudi Menuhin Music Guides*, ed. Sir Keith Falkner. London: Macdonald and Co.

White, Ernest G. (1938), *Sinus Tone Production*. London: J. M. Dent and Sons Ltd.

www.youtube.com. The authors also recommend that there is much good material to be heard and seen on the YouTube internet site.

INDEX OF LISTENING SUGGESTIONS

PHOTOGRAPH AND ILLUSTRATION CREDITS

AUTHOR BIOGRAPHIES

Jane Streeton and Philip Raymond
Photographer: Oliver King

JANE STREETON studied at the Royal College of Music where she graduated with honours and was a winner of the Clara Butt Award.

Jane has sung as soloist in opera and concert internationally and in the UK has worked with the English National Opera and the English Bach Festival at the Royal Opera House. She sings largely with British touring opera companies and has performed principal roles in the operas of Mozart, Puccini, Verdi, Wagner, Britten, Gilbert & Sullivan, Johann Strauss and others. She has sung for Opera Restor'd and has recorded with them on Hyperion.

Festival appearances include Buxton, Edinburgh and abroad at the Utrecht Early Music Festival and the Barbados Festival. In concert she has sung at the Purcell Room, the Wigmore Hall and as soloist with the Royal Philharmonic Orchestra and the London Gala Orchestra in their Viennese Spectaculars.

At RADA, Jane is Co-ordinator of the Singing Team and teaches on the BA in Acting, Musical Theatre Short Courses and for Youth Workshops. She has also taught at the Guildford School of Acting and Webber Douglas Academy. Jane has given masterclasses in Rome, in Sydney at NIDA, at Monash University in Melbourne, at the Boris Schukin Theatre School in Moscow and at Lewis and Clark University in Portland, Oregon.

Jane has worked as singing coach and vocal adviser for film and with the BBC, in West End Musicals, at the Royal Shakespeare Company, the National Theatre and Shakespeare's Globe.

PHILIP RAYMOND was born in Merthyr Tydfil in South Wales and began his musical training in St David's Cathedral, Pembrokeshire where he was to become head chorister. One of the highlights of his early career was singing as treble soloist in the Mozart Requiem in the Lambeth Conference of 1974 in Canterbury Cathedral in memoriam of Pope John Paul.

He sang as soloist and chorister with the National Youth Choir for many years before entering the Royal College of Music in 1989, where his studies spanned six years on the performers and advanced performers courses. His singing teachers were Lyndon van der Pump and Edward Brooks; Alastair Graham was his piano teacher and vocal coach.

Philip has been a tenor soloist in recital, oratorio and opera in the UK and abroad performing with groups such as Mecklenburgh Opera Company and The Rossini Society. He has appeared in many major concert halls and Cathedrals.

He chose to develop his career as a teacher rather than as a performer, and was appointed to the Webber Douglas Academy, where he became Head of Music, and then as a tutor at the RADA from 1989. He also maintains a considerable private studio. With Jane Streeton he has given masterclasses for the Boris Schukin Theatre School, Moscow.

Philip is deputy organist of St Stevens Church, Watling Street, St Albans, and a keen and competitive cyclist, regularly competing for his club, the Welwyn Wheelers in regional cyclo cross events and on the velodrome at Welwyn Garden City.

If you would like to keep in touch with Jane and Philip and Singing on Stage, please follow them on Twitter @streetonraymond.